GW01220991

GRASS HILL

Translations from the Oriental Classics

GRASS HILL
Poems and Prose
by the Japanese Monk Gensei

Translated by Burton Watson

Columbia University Press
New York
1983

The Japan Foundation, through a special grant,
has assisted the Press in publishing this volume.

Library of Congress Cataloging in Publication Data

Nichisei, 1623–1668.
　Grass hill.

　(Translations from the oriental classics)
　Verse and prose.
　Translation of: Sōzanshū.
　Includes bibliographical references.
　I. Watson, Burton, 1925–　. II. Title. II. Series.
PL2720.I25S6　1983　　　895.1'8　　　82-19744
ISBN 0-231-05606-0

Columbia University Press
New York　　　Guildford, Surrey

Copyright © 1983 Columbia University Press
All rights reserved
Printed in the United States of America

Clothbound editions of Columbia University Press books
are Smyth-sewn and printed on permanent and durable
acid-free paper.

Translations from the Oriental Classics

Editorial Board

Wm. Theodore de Bary, Chairman

C. T. Hsia
Barbara Stoler Miller
Burton Watson

Donald Keene
Edward Seidensticker
Philip B. Yampolsky

CONTENTS

Introduction   ix

Translator's Note   xxxi

Grass Hill
    Poetry   1
    Prose Selections   81

Appendix: Gensei's Japanese Poetry   113

INTRODUCTION

JAPAN IN THE early decades of the seventeenth century was recovering from an extended period of internal strife and foreign intercourse that, in cultural terms, had been both extremely stimulating and extremely disruptive. During this period some of the arts, such as painting and architecture, flourishing under the patronage of the powerful warlords of the time and stimulated by influences from abroad, had reached levels of splendor they would seldom achieve again. But literature and learning, which in general require less turbulent conditions in order to thrive, had suffered considerably in the century or more of turmoil. The task of the seventeenth century was to mend the breaks that had occurred in the literary and scholarly traditions of the nation and to redirect attention to peaceful pursuits.

One of the fields of learning that had flourished at various times in the past was that of Chinese studies. In the early period of cultural contact between China and Japan, particularly from the seventh to the ninth centuries, the Japanese devoted themselves enthusiastically to the study of Chinese thought and literature, frequently composing original works of poetry and prose in Chinese. A second great era of interest in Chinese studies occurred around the thirteenth to the fifteenth centuries, when many Japanese Buddhist monks, particularly those of the Zen sect, went to

China to study. The poetry and prose in Chinese produced by Zen monks of the time, known as *Gozan bungaku* or the "Literature of the Five Mountains" in reference to the major Zen temples of Kyoto and Kamakura, reached a high level of technical excellence, and for a time Chinese influence was once more dominant in Japanese culture. But the great Zen monasteries, which had served as bastions of learning, were badly damaged in the civil wars of the late fifteenth and sixteenth centuries, and little literature of importance in Chinese was produced during that period.

The Tokugawa shogunate restored peace and unity to the country at the beginning of the seventeenth century, thus providing the atmosphere of social stability needed for the revival of learning. In time the shogunate also adopted the Chinese Neo-Confucian philosophy as the official doctrine of the state and took steps to encourage Confucian studies. Meanwhile, a number of private individuals, some of them scholarly minded samurai whose interest was mainly in Confucianism, others Buddhist monks or members of the court aristocracy, labored on their own to restore literature and learning to its former state. One such figure who played an important role in the literary renaissance was Gensei (1623–1668), a Buddhist monk of the Nichiren sect, whose poetry and prose, most of it written in Chinese, is the subject of this volume.

GENSEI'S LIFE

Gensei was born in the second month of 1623 at Ichijō, east of Horikawa in Kyoto. He was a son of a family named Ishii which for generations had served as officials in the households of the Kyoto nobility, and thus was heir to the old cultural traditions of the capital. During the period of social turmoil, Gensei's father Motoyoshi (1572–1658), departing from the family tradition, ventured into military life, entering the service of the powerful warlord Mōri Terumoto (1553–1625). He took part in the famous battle of Sekigahara in 1600, but unfortunately on the losing side, and therafter gradually withdrew from active life. Gensei's mother came from the area of Ishiyama in Ōmi province at the south end of Lake Biwa.

Gensei was the child of his parents' old age, a fact that greatly affected his relationship to them. He is often described as the fifth son, though in fact he was the fourth and last. The misleading description derives from the fact that his father adopted a son from another family to carry on the Kujō branch of the Ishii family, and this adopted son is listed in genealogies as though he were an elder brother of Gensei.

Gensei had two sisters, both older. The elder entered the service of Ii Naotaka (1589–1659), lord of the castle of Hikone in Ōmi east of Lake Biwa. She became Ii's favorite concubine and bore him a son, Naosumi (1625–1676), who in time became lord of the domain and a high official in the Tokugawa shogunate. Gensei's second sister married a samurai in the service of that branch of the Tokugawa family that served as lords of the castle of Nagoya in Owari. Thus Gensei had important family connections not only with the old court aristocracy, but with the newly established Tokugawa military government as well. Because of his sister's influence, Gensei's eldest brother Motohide (1608–1682) entered the service of the Ii family, serving three lords of Hikone in succession and enjoying great favor and affluence. Gensei's two other brothers, who were perhaps in fact half brothers, became Buddhist monks, though little is known of them; the elder died at an early age.

In view of these close connections with the Ii family, it is not surprising that Gensei should have been sent at the age of seven to stay with his eldest brother in Hikone and get a taste of samurai life. He returned to Kyoto two years later, but in 1635, at the age of twelve, once more went to

Hikone and formally entered the service of the daimyo Ii Naotaka. He remained in service until 1641, accompanying his lord to Edo at least once, but was taken sick in Edo and returned to Kyoto or Hikone for a year of rest and recuperation. Already the ill health that was to plague him the rest of his life had made its dour appearance.

The earliest biography of Gensei, written in Chinese in 1669 by a Zen monk of Kennin-ji named Tsūken and prefaced to editions of Gensei's works, contains several brief episodes intended to illustrate his precocity as a child and his early disposition for learning. These I believe may be passed over in silence. Anecdotes of this type are such an indispensable element in conventional Chinese and Japanese hagiography that, if they had not existed, we may be sure they would have been invented for the occasion.

The following anecdote, however, cannot be so lightly dismissed. After mentioning Gensei's illness in 1641 and his subsequent year of recuperation, Tsūken states: "He went with his mother on a trip to Wake in Izumi, where he bowed before a statue of Nichiren Shōnin and took the following three vows. 'First, I will without fail become a monk. Second, since my father and mother are advanced in years, I will serve them with utmost filial devotion. Third, I will read the three major writings of T'ien-t'ai.' "[1] Gensei was faithful to his three vows, and his later years were in fact devoted to the concerns that they suggest: the calling of a

---

1. The most important works of T'ien-t'ai or Chih-i (538–597), the virtual founder of T'ien-t'ai Buddhism in China. They are the *Fa-hua hsüan-i, Fa-hua wen-chü,* and *Mo-ho chih-kuan,* all commentaries on the Lotus Sutra. These works, along with the Lotus Sutra itself, constitute the philosophical basis of both the Tendai and Nichiren sects of Buddhism in Japan. The statue Gensei saw was said to have been carved out of a single piece of wood by Nichiren himself at the time of his exile in Izu in 1261–63. Later the statue was divided into three parts and given to his disciples. The temple Gensei visited, Myōsen-ji (in Wake, in present-day Izumi Fuchū), preserves the lower part of the statue; the head and torso portions are preserved elsewhere.

Buddhist monk, the care of his parents, and the pursuit of learning and literature.

With his new interest in Buddhism, Gensei began attending a series of daily lectures on the Lotus Sutra given by a Vinaya Master of Sennyū-ji, a Shingon temple in the southeast suburbs of Kyoto, staying in a nearby inn. Deeply moved by what he heard, he expressed a desire to enter religious life, but was advised by the Vinaya Master that he was too young for such a step. The next year, his health apparently mended, he returned to the service of the Ii family in Hikone.

In 1647, at the age of 24, he left the Ii family for the last time and returned to Kyoto, more than ever determined to fulfill his vow to become a monk. The following year, with the consent of his parents, he entered Myōken-ji, also called Ryūge-in, the oldest Nichiren sect temple in Kyoto, and became a disciple of Nichihō, the head priest.[2] His parents at the time were living at the Kujō residence of the family at the far southern edge of the city, but Gensei arranged for them to move into a rented house at Ichijō close to the tem-

2. The Nichiren or Lotus sect was founded by the Japanese monk Nichiren (1222–1282), who is often referred to by the honorary titles Shōnin or Daishōnin. In his youth he studied Tendai Buddhism and developed a great admiration for the Chinese Tendai patriarch Chih-i or T'ien-t'ai (see note above) and the Japanese Tendai patriarch Saichō or Dengyō (767–822). Like these men, he regarded the Lotus Sutra as the highest embodiment of Buddhist teaching and the ideal means to enlightenment, and saw himself as a votary of the Lotus Sutra whose mission was to propagate its doctrines. He considered all other forms of Buddhism as a kind of slander directed against the Lotus Sutra and called on the government authorities to suppress the Shingon, Pure Land, Zen, and Ritsu sects, which enjoyed wide popularity in his time, and to support his teachings, predicting that failure to do so would bring disaster upon the Japanese nation. The Nichiren sect accordingly places great emphasis upon the study of the Lotus Sutra and of T'ien-t'ai's exegetical writings, as well as Nichiren's own letters and doctrinal writings in Chinese and Japanese. It also advocates the chanting of the formula *Nam-myōhō-renge-kyō*, which means "Hail to the Lotus Sutra!" but is believed to possess mystic power far transcending the meaning of the words. In the centuries following Nichiren's death, the sect split into a number of contending factions.

ple so that he could visit them daily even during his period of religious training. Thus, whether the story of the three vows is true or not, it was clear from the beginning that, although Gensei had withdrawn from secular life, he had no intention of cutting off his ties with his parents.

Gensei, as his later life indicated, was temperamentally well fitted for the pursuit of scholarly and literary activities. His decision to become a monk, aside from its indisputably sincere religious motives, may well have been dictated by his desire for greater leisure to pursue such activities. Moreover, the uncertain state of his health probably convinced him that he was not suited for continued duty in the service of the Ii family. Finally, he no doubt wished to make sure that his parents would be properly cared for, a task that his eldest brother, committed to service of the Ii family in Hikone, could not be expected to look after.

Such considerations would seem to offer reason enough for Gensei's decision to enter religious life. But the world craves more striking and colorful motives for those who turn their back on its pleasures, and it is not surprising that, in Gensei's case, legend has obligingly supplied them. Though there is no hint of any such thing in his writings, rumor held that his decision to become a monk was precipitated by an unhappy love affair. According to one version of the story, while in Edo in attendance on his lord he visited the Yoshiwara pleasure quarter and fell in love with a high-ranking courtesan. The two pledged undying fidelity, but shortly after, the courtesan committed suicide because of some other affair. Gensei's grief, it is reported, drove him to seek solace in religion.

In view of Gensei's impressive family connections and the fact that he seems to have been a good-looking young man who enjoyed considerable favor and fortune, there is nothing completely implausible about the story. One should note, however, that the Japanese have a penchant for attaching romantic episodes of this kind to the names of their eminent men of religion, as though to draw attention to the feet of clay. In any event, the tale appears to have gained wide credence in Kyoto after Gensei's death, and it is said that young couples desiring to marry would visit his grave to pray for a speedy realization of their hopes.

Gensei adopted two religious names, Nissei and Gensei. The first borrows the Nichi element from the name of Nichiren Shōnin, a common practice among priests of the Nichiren sect, and corresponds to a personal name. The second is simply another reading of his adult name Motomasa, which uses the element Gen or Moto from his father's name Motoyoshi, an element that derives originally from the name of his father's onetime lord Mōri Terumoto. In addition, he used the literary names Myōshi, Fukashigi, and Taidō.

Gensei appears to have continued his religious training under Nichihō until 1655, when his teacher left Kyoto to move to Hommon-ji, a temple near Edo in Ikegami, the place where Nichiren Shōnin died and an important center of the Nichiren sect. Thereafter Gensei moved to the location in Fukakusa south of Kyoto where he was to live for the remainder of his life, building a small residence there called the Shōshin-an.

The Fushimi area, of which Fukakusa is a part, was no doubt fairly well populated at the time, since one of the main roads running south from Kyoto passed through it and it is the site of many important shrines and temples. Gensei built his residence somewhat east of the main road, on a small hill called Kusayama or Grass Hill. A little to the north is the much larger hill on which the famous Fushimi Inari Shrine is located, one of the most important Shinto shrines in the Kyoto area. Behind him ran a range of hills, the south end of Higashiyama, that separated him from the Yamashina valley to the east, while to the west flowed the Katsura and Kamo rivers, the latter plied by boats carrying travelers downstream to Osaka and the sea. Gensei was thus less than an hour's walk from the capital and close to means of transportation by palanquin and boat, but at the same time in a pleasantly quiet and wooded area. Just why he chose to settle in this particular spot is not known, though it is possible that his family had connections with the area, since it formed part of the estate of the powerful Kujō family in which his own family residence was located.

The following year, 1656, Gensei arranged for his parents to move from their Kujō residence to his new establishment. They lived there for the remainder of their lives, his father dying in 1658 at the age of 86, his mother in 1667 at 86. Thus Gensei fulfilled his vow to look after them in their old age. In addition, he had several disciples, and also took in a number of young boys who were sent to him by other temples for an education, giving them regular instruction in the various aspects of Buddhism. In 1661 he built a separate residence for his mother, the Yōju-an, and a hall of worship, formally establishing a temple under the name Zuikō-ji, the Temple of Auspicious Light. It remains in existence today, its little hall of worship still roofed with thatch as it was in Gensei's day. Presumably these various buildings were constructed with funds from his own family, or possibly from the Ii family. In his writings he describes himself as the son of a poor family, but this would seem to be little more than literary convention.

Gensei was ill a good deal of the time, and made frequent trips to a medical practitioner named Sano Yūken in Takatsuki, a castle town between Kyoto and Osaka on the Yodo River, journeying there by boat.[3] There he underwent acupuncture and moxa treatment and took doses of medi-

---

3. Gensei traveled by boat or palanquin much of the time. Probably because of his frail health, he was not very good at lengthy trips on foot, and his account of a visit to Iwama Temple in Ōmi reveals that he was often torn between the desire to visit a place and fear that his legs would not get him there (Sōzanshū ch. 5, p. 97). On the trip to Mt. Minobu and Edo that he made with his mother in 1659, his legs gave out on the second day and he had to make the remainder of the journey on horse.

cine. In his later years he made two trips to the hot springs at Arima near present-day Kobe, the baths there proving helpful. The exact nature of his illness is unknown. Tuberculosis of the lungs is an obvious possibility, particularly since he mentions coughing up blood in a letter written in his late years.[4] But that does not seem to be the whole story, as he repeatedly speaks of suffering attacks of lumbago brought on by the dampness in his hill retreat, and at one time of a seige of boils. In any event, it is abundantly clear from his letters and poems that he was ill and in pain a great deal of the time. As in the case of Masaoka Shiki (1867–1902), another poet who battled all his life against illness, one can only be amazed at Gensei's output and the strength and resilience of his spirit.

Gensei's poetry and shorter prose works in Chinese are collected in a volume entitled *Sōzanshū* or "Grass Hill Collection." The book is in two parts, an initial section in 20 chapters followed by a 10-chapter continuation. The first part was presumably compiled by Gensei himself and the latter added by Gensei's disciple Emyō (1642–1717) when he prepared the work for publication in 1674. Both sections consist of prose works arranged by genre—introductions, letters, travel pieces, biographies, etc.—followed by poems. There are a total of 328 prose pieces and over 1,000 poems. The poems in the latter part, which date from the last three years of Gensei's life, are arranged chronologically. But those in the first part are arranged according to poetic form, e.g., 5-character old style, 7-character old style, etc. Thus, unless a poem in this section includes a heading that states the date of composition, it is difficult to determine exactly when a given work was written, and hence to discuss stylistic development.

---

4. *Sōzanshū* ch. 25, p. 462. For information on the edition cited, see Translator's Note, p. xxxii. Hereafter *Sōzanshū* will be referred to by the abbreviation *SZS*.

One of the earliest datable poems, and the one that appears to have constituted Gensei's literary debut, was written on New Year's Day of 1656, shortly after he moved to Fukakusa, and describes his new home. I quote it here in the translation by Donald Keene given in his discussion of the poet in *World Within Walls*.[5]

My New House

Nobody knows yet about my new house.
This spring I came here alone, quite by chance.
When I washed my pots I discovered the spring water
    was hot;
When I read the sutras I noticed how much time I had
    before evening.
Haze and clouds shut in my quiet door;
Fragrant grasses sprout outside my rough gate.
Pines and bamboos have found their own place;
Now in the woods and hills the snow begins to melt.

The poem, we are told, was quickly passed around among the literary circles of the capital and "ran up the price of paper," as the conventional phrase has it. It is cast in the difficult *lü-shih*, or regulated verse form, which requires strict verbal parallelism in the two middle couplets and tonal parallelism throughout. Gensei's ability to fulfill these prosodic requirements, and in particular the neat parallelism of the middle couplets, are no doubt what inspired admiration rather than any striking originality of thought or expression.

As the reader will see from the selection that follows, Gensei wrote in a variety of poetic forms. Some of his works have extensive prose introductions describing the circumstances of composition, while others, such as those written

---

5. *World Within Walls: Japanese Literature of the Pre-Modern Era, 1600–1867* (New York: Holt, Rinehart & Winston, 1976), p. 540.

on journeys or outings, can be matched up with prose pieces that describe the same outing. Some were written to his disciples or students, others to his friends, of whom he had many among the Buddhist clergy and Confucian scholars of the capital area. Though he wrote some works of a specifically doctrinal nature, the majority of his poems deal with his daily life and activities. This highly personal quality is one of the outstanding characteristics of his poetry and the chief reason that it remains of interest to us today.

His miscellaneous prose works are more varied in nature. Many are religious pieces of a specialized nature such as grave inscriptions, inscriptions for temple bells, or biographies of eminent clergymen which were no doubt written on request. Others, such as the travel pieces, letters, and informal essays, are more personal in content, and it is mainly works of this latter type that have been translated here.

Classical Chinese was to the Buddhist clergy of premodern Japan what Latin was to their Christian counterparts in medieval Europe: the language in which they read the sacred scriptures, and in which most exegetical and devotional works were written. It is perfectly understandable, therefore, why men like Gensei should have placed such great emphasis upon the study of Chinese and have employed it to compose poetry and religious pieces such as those I have mentioned above.[6] It is less clear, however, why he should have gone so far as to write personal letters in Chinese. In the case of letters addressed to his disciples, the reason may

---

6. Gensei complains in a letter that the boys studying under him want to begin lecturing on the Dharma and spreading the teachings "before they even know the *go* or *kan* pronunciation of the Chinese characters or whether the characters belong to the level or deflected tone categories!" He compares this to a bodhisattva trying to enlighten others before he himself has attained enlightenment. As may be seen from this, Gensei considered a sound knowledge of the Chinese language, including Chinese poetics, to be absolutely indispensable to anyone hoping to be a leader in religious life (*SZS* ch. 2, p. 46).

have been partly pedagogical, though it is hard not to tax him with a certain degree of literary affectation. I would merely point out that the Japanese epistolary style in use in his time, with its tedious repetitions of honorifics, is notoriously long-winded and space-consuming. Chinese epistolary style, to be sure, has flowery phrases of its own, but it is still capable of saying much more in less space than Japanese. It is possible, therefore, that Gensei wrote letters in Chinese in part for reasons of speed and economy.

In 1659, the year after his father's death, Gensei set off with his mother for a journey to Mount Minobu in the province of Kai, the place where Nichiren Shōnin spent his last years and a sacred spot to members of the Nichiren sect. The trip was undertaken at the instigation of Gensei's mother, one purpose being to deposit some of his father's ashes on the holy mountain.

On the way, the pair stopped in Nagoya to visit Gensei's younger sister who, as mentioned earlier, was married to a samurai in the service of Nagoya Castle. At their home Gensei was introduced to a Chinese emigré named Ch'en Yüan-yün (1587–1671). There is some doubt as to where Ch'en was born and when and under what circumstances he came to Japan. He was a highly educated man and in time became acquainted with many of the eminent scholars and government leaders of Japan. He appears to have remained in Japan in order to avoid the turmoil that accompanied the downfall of the Ming dynasty. In his late years he enjoyed the patronage of the lord of Nagoya Castle. By the time Gensei met him, Ch'en had lived in Japan for many years and spoke fluent Japanese, though with a pronounced accent.[7]

Though there was a great disparity in their ages—Ch'en was 72 at the time, Gensei 36—the two seem to have hit it

---

7. For a detailed study of the data concerning Ch'en, see Komatsubara Tō, *Chin Gempin no kenkyū* (Tokyo: Yūzan Kaku, 1962).

off immediately. In the succeeding years, they often exchanged letters and poems, and Ch'en spent much time with Gensei whenever he had occasion to visit Kyoto.[8] One such occasion they spent together reading the works of several Ming writers. Gensei sent his poems to Ch'en for criticism, and the latter, as we shall see when we come to examine Gensei's views on literature, did much to influence the younger man's poetic style.

After the stop in Nagoya, Gensei and his mother went on to Mount Minobu, and from there to Edo, where Gensei visited his old teacher Nichihō at Ikegami. On his way back to Kyoto, he stopped once more in Nagoya and visited with Ch'en. Gensei compiled an account of the journey in Japanese, the *Minobu no michi no ki* in two chapters, which contains a number of poems in Chinese and Japanese that he wrote along the way. It was published in 1663.

This was Gensei's last extended journey. In the remaining years, he contented himself with outings to nearby spots such as Uji or Yamashina, or traveled to Takatsuki or Arima for health reasons. In 1661 his disciple Giō, whom he had no doubt counted upon to succeed him as head of the temple, died at the age of 37. The moving biography which he wrote of Giō, translated on pp. 93–99 below, not only indicates the affection he felt for his disciple, but reveals much about his own thinking, particularly his deep concern with the ideal of filial devotion. In 1665 he acquired another disciple, Emyō, to whom he increasingly entrusted supervision of temple affairs and whom he in time named as his religious heir. By this time he was widely known as a man of letters and an authority on Buddhism and Chinese and Japanese literature and had many visitors, among them the famous Confucian scholar Kumazawa Banzan (1619–1691).

8. In 1663 Gensei compiled the poems they had exchanged into a two-chapter work entitled *Gen Gen shōwashū* or "Poems Exchanged between Yüan and Gen," to which each wrote a brief preface praising the other's works. It was printed the same year.

His mother spent much of her time alone in her room engaged in religious devotions, hard of hearing but otherwise in sound health. Gensei's health, however, continued to decline, and he began to be seriously concerned that he might die before she did. She was taken ill in the fall of 1667, and Gensei, largely through an act of sheer will power, managed to stay well enough to nurse her until her death in the last month of the year. As soon as the funeral proceedings were over, he hurried off to Takatsuki in a last effort to regain his own health. He soon realized the futility of any further attempts at medical treatment, however, and returned to the temple to put his affairs in order. He died on the 18th day of the second month of 1668, a little over two months after his mother. In accordance with his instructions, he was buried at the temple in a grave marked only by three stalks of bamboo. It is said that one stalk was dedicated to the Lotus Sutra, one to his parents, and one to the salvation of humankind.

GENSEI'S LITERARY VIEWS

Gensei's religious and other specialized writings, which run to over ten titles, consist of short works of two or three chapters dealing mainly with the lives of Buddhist priests or recluses, exegeses of Buddhist texts, or devotional works, some written in Japanese for the benefit of his mother. In addition, there is a slim collection of his Japanese poems in *tanka* form, the *Sōzan wakashū,* published in 1672 and somewhat expanded in later editions, though the total number of poems is relatively small. A recently discovered collection of early poems brings the total of his Japanese poems to about 250.[9] It is obvious, therefore, that Gensei's reputation

---

9. See Shimabara Yasuo, *"Fukakusa Gensei Shōnin Wakashū ni tsuite, Bungaku ronsō* no. 48, Tōyō daigaku kokubun kenkyūshitsu 1973, pp. 83–92.

as a poet and prose writer must rest mainly on the thirty chapters that make up the *Sōzanshū*.

Among the earliest critical comments on Gensei's work are those put forward by Emura Hokkai (1713–1788) in chapter three of his *Nihon shishi* or "History of Japanese *Kanshi*." "Among the masters of *kanshi* poetry of the Kambun era (1661–72)," he writes, "there are none who can surpass Ishikawa Jōzan and the priest Gensei." And later, speaking of Gensei, he remarks, "Although his poetry is not particularly lofty in tone, it is marked by clear and realistic ideas and content." To better understand the rather faint praise of the latter statement, we must consider for a moment the view of poetry that Gensei espoused.

As mentioned previously, it is difficult to discuss Gensei's early literary development because so few of the poems of his younger years can be dated with certainty. We do not even know when, where, or with whom he studied the writing of poetry in Chinese, though he must certainly have had his teachers. From the facts available to us, it would appear that the most momentous event in his stylistic development was his meeting with Ch'en Yüan-yün in Nagoya in 1659.

At that time, Ch'en recommended to him the works of a late Ming poet named Yüan Hung-tao (1568–1610). When Gensei returned from his journey, he searched the Kyoto bookstores and located a copy of Yüan's collected works, the *Yüan Chung-lang ch'üan-chi*, which had most likely reached Kyoto by way of the Chinese traders who regularly called at Nagasaki. In a poem translated on p. 4, we see him delightedly poring over his new find.[10]

---

10. The praise that Yüan Hung-tao lavishes on the popular Chinese novel *Shui-hu chuan* (*Water Margin*) in time led Gensei to search for that work as well. In a letter to the Confucian scholar and bibliophile Ukai Yukinobu (1616–1664), he mentions that he found it listed in the catalogue of a Kyoto bookseller, but when he asked for the book, he was told that someone had already bought it and taken it away. The bookseller was unable to identify

Before the time of Yüan Hung-tao, Ming poetry had been dominated by men of the so-called archaic movement who placed great emphasis upon the formal elements of poetry and advocated careful imitation of the masterpieces of the past, especially the works of the great T'ang poets such as Li Po and Tu Fu. Yüan, along with his two brothers, who were also poets, reacted strongly against such views. Instead, drawing on the ideas of the highly individualistic thinker Li Chih, they stressed the personal and emotional aspects of poetry. A key term in their critical vocabulary was *hsing-ling* or *seirei*, which James J. Y. Liu has translated as "personal nature" or "native sensibility."[11] For them, true poetry is that which embodies this inner sensibility of the individual, which gives expression to emotions that flow freely and irrepressibly from the heart of the writer.

Gensei's acquaintance with the poetry and poetic theory of Yüan Hung-tao seems to have resulted less in any drastic redirection of his own work than in a reinforcing of tastes and tendencies already present in it. Thus, for example, in a short piece written for his disciple Giō in 1658, a year before his meeting with Ch'en Yüan-yün, he advises,

---

the purchaser, and we do not know whether Gensei ever succeeded in getting hold of a copy of the novel or not (*SZS* ch. 3, p. 63). The number and variety of Chinese books in the possession of Gensei's temple suggests that he had one of the largest private libraries of Chinese books in Japan in his time. See the catalogue of the temple's Chinese books in Munemasa Isoo, "Gensei," *Bungaku gogaku* no. 58 (December 1970), pp. 74–78.

11. See James J. Y. Liu, *The Art of Chinese Poetry* (Chicago: University of Chicago Press, 1962), pp. 73–74, and *Chinese Theories of Literature* (Chicago: University of Chicago Press, 1975), pp. 78–81. For an excellent selection of poetry and prose by Yüan Hung-tao and his brothers in translation, along with an introduction discussing their literary views, see Jonathan Chaves, *Pilgrim of the Clouds: Poems and Essays from Ming China* (Tokyo/New York: Weatherhill, 1978). See also Hing-shui Hung, *Yüan Hung-tao* (Boston: Twayne, 1981). For a discussion of Li Chih, see Wm. Theodore de Bary, "Individualism and Humanitarianism in Late Ming Thought," in *Self and Society in Ming Thought*, Wm. T. de Bary and the Conference on Ming Thought (New York: Columbia University Press, 1970) especially pp. 188–225.

"When feelings overwhelm you and you can't drive them away even though you try, then write a poem to describe them" (*SZS* ch. 1, p. 26). This, of course, with its emphasis on the emotional and irrepressible nature of poetry, accords exactly with the view of Yüan Hung-tao.

But even though Gensei may instinctively have held views similar to those of Yüan and his group, the concept of *seirei* or native sensibility gave him a convenient label for summing up his ideas, and he adopted it with enthusiasm. Thus, in a letter to Enchō, a clergyman of southern Kii, he speaks warmly of the importance of *seirei* over mere imitation in literature and praises the writings of his correspondent for the fact that "they all flow out of *seirei*" (*SZS* ch. 2, pp. 47–48). And in a poem entitled "Impromptu" written in 1667, he states:

> Poems bring forth the best in one's inner nature (*seirei*);
> they're irrepressible—who can stop them?
> (*SZS* ch. 23, p. 427)

In a prose piece dating from his late years, he expands the concept of *seirei* until it becomes a kind of mystic religious concept, declaring, "He who embodies *seirei* can become the master of all the ten thousand dharmas, . . . and with it can purify the Buddha lands and bring enlightenment to all sentient beings" (*SZS* ch. 27, pp. 524–25.)

While indulging in such flights of metaphysical rhetoric, Gensei could at the same time deliver very down-to-earth advice concerning literature, as when he counsels a friend that there is only one way to become a good writer: "Read diligently and write a lot. Then you won't have to wait for other people to point it out to you—you yourself can see what is good or bad" (*SZS* ch. 29, p. 567). And for all his references to expressive or metaphysical theories of literature, his overall conception of literature was, like that of nearly all Japanese of the time who were involved in

Chinese studies, in the end basically moral. Morality is the root, he insists, literature the branch; one is fundamental, the other secondary. And, since literature in his view is an expression of the inner nature of the individual, it follows that a person of sound moral qualities will quite naturally produce writings of worth (*SZS* ch. 29, pp. 566, 568).

Emura Hokkai, as we have seen earlier, pairs Gensei with Ishikawa Jōzan (1583–1672) as one of the two most outstanding *kanshi* poets of the mid-seventeenth century. As may be seen from Ishikawa's dates, he was forty years older than Gensei. In his youth he won distinction as a warrior in battle, but with the restoration of peace, he devoted himself to Confucian studies and the writing of poetry in Chinese. In 1636 he retired to a country house in the hills northeast of Kyoto that was strikingly similar in setting to Gensei's retreat southeast of the city, and he lived there for the remainder of his life. Like Gensei, he admired the works of Yüan Hung-tao, though on the whole he tended to follow the theories of those Ming critics who advocated archaism.[12]

Given the close-knit character of Kyoto literary and scholarly circles, the two men could hardly have been unaware of each other's existence. In fact, Ch'en Yüan-yün and Ishikawa had been friends for some years, so that if Ishikawa and Gensei were not acquainted, Ch'en could easily have introduced them. And yet Ishikawa and Gensei do not appear to have exchanged poems, as one might expect of two men so avidly devoted to the writing of *kanshi*, and in fact neither makes the slightest mention of the other. Why two such eminent men of letters should so studiously ignore each other is unclear. One suspects there must be some intriguing story here, but so far no one has ferreted out the facts.

---

12. On Ishikawa's theory and practice of poetry, see Matsushita Tadashi, *Edo jidai no shifū shiron* ("*Kanshi* Theory and Style in the Edo Period") (Tokyo: Meiji shoin, 1969), pp. 261–76.

Though the expressive and individualistic view of literature espoused by Yüan Hung-tao and his brothers enjoyed great popularity for a time in late Ming China, it was on the whole rejected by writers of the early Ch'ing dynasty (1644–1911). This fact may help to explain why no Japanese writers of *kanshi* followed Ishikawa and Gensei in taking an interest in Yüan's poetry and the *hsing-ling* or *seirei* theory of literature. Instead, mainly through the influence of men like Ogyū Sorai (1668–1728) and Arai Hakuseki (1657–1725), Japanese *kanshi* came strongly under the influence of the Ming archaist or formalist school, the very group against whom Yüan had rebelled, formalist views having enjoyed a revival of influence in China at the time. This is no doubt why Emura Hokkai, writing under the sway of such views, could look back at the poetry of men like Gensei and Ishikawa and complain that it was not sufficiently "lofty in tone" or, as he says of Ishikawa's work, "often fails to avoid common-sounding effects" (*Nihon shishi* ch. 3). It was only when the *hsing-ling* concept of poetry regained standing in China through the popularizing efforts of Yüan Mei (1716–1798) that it was reintroduced to Japan, this time to replace archaism as the dominant theory among *kanshi* writers. Thus Gensei, with his personal approach and attention to the scenes of everyday life, became a kind of spiritual ancestor to the late Edo period *kanshi* poets, though there was no direct line of literary transmission linking them.

It is something of an irony that Gensei, who on the whole lived such a serene and drama-less life, should have chosen to make his daily experiences the principal subject of his poetry, when other writers such as the Zen monks of Gozan literature, who lived through violent strife and social upheaval, had written for the most part in a studiedly detached and impersonal style. The surprising thing about Gensei's poetry is that, in spite of the rather limited range of experience it deals with, it nevertheless manages to be almost consistently interesting, mainly because of its careful observation, honesty of presentation, and underlying air of religious conviction. True, he harps a bit too often on the secluded and "otherwordly" nature of his existence, particularly for someone who lived only five minutes' walk from a bustling highway. Perhaps, however, the reclusion he is talking about is less physical than mental and spiritual, as he suggests in the lines, "Not that this is a place deep in clouds, / but in my heart I have mountains of my own" (*SZS* ch. 16, p. 266). In any event, we are willing to forgive such minor lapses into affectation because of the overwhelming sincerity and warmth of his work as a whole. One is tempted to say he is proof of his own dictum that sound character produces sound writing.

Biographers all remark on the austerity of Gensei's manner of life and the care with which he observed the rules of monastic discipline. He was a strict teetotaler and forbade any drinking among the members of his religious group, though he discovered to his distress that this prohibition was not always observed when he was absent from the premises. However, his wide circle of friends among clergymen of other sects and manifest admiration for the Chinese Zen poet Shih-te or Jittoku suggest that, though utterly sincere in his own religious convictions, he was at the same time tolerant of the differing beliefs and practices of others, something for which the Nichiren sect as a whole has hardly been noteworthy. He was apparently concerned with mending breaches, not widening them.

This is nowhere better seen than in his efforts to reconcile Buddhist and Confucian concerns and values. "The Great Way knows no Confucians or Buddhists; / men are all of them brothers," he declares in a poem written for the sons of a noted Confucian scholar (*SZS* ch. 21, p. 367). This concept of the essential unity of the two creeds had been voiced often enough in the past, both in China and Japan. But Gensei, with his abiding concern for the ideal of filial devotion, attempted to make it a reality in his own life. The very essence of becoming a monk has traditionally been that one cuts off ties of kinship, as the term used to describe it, *shukke* or "leaving the family," unequivocally indicates. Gensei refused to be bound by this definition but followed his own convictions, whether they conformed to tradition or not. To emphasize his point, he even compiled a work, the *Shakushi nijūshi kō*, containing biographies of twenty-four Chinese and Japanese Buddhist monks noted for their filial piety. His single-minded devotion to his parents, perhaps more than any other quality in his life or work, has inspired the admiration of his countrymen. Like his near contemporary, the Confucian scholar Nakae Tōju (1608–1648), he has been remembered above all as a dutiful son.[13]

Whether that is how a Buddhist monk ought to be remembered, it is probably pointless to ask. Gensei was a man of independent-minded personality, and the fact that so much of that personality comes across in his poetry and prose is, as I have said, what gives his writings lasting interest. At the same time, he was honest enough to admit that, although he may have done his duty by his parents, he had not necessarily done it by the world as a whole. As he states in a piece translated on p. 74, his hope was that in his next existence he could use his hard-won enlightenment "to save as many living beings as I can."

---

13. In 1692, when Tokugawa Mitsukuni (1628–1700), the lord of the domain of Mito and an important cultural leader, visited the site in Minatogawa where the warrior Kusunoki Masashige was purportedly buried and left a marker with the inscription "Ah, the resting place of Kusunoki, a loyal subject!," he proposed a similar inscription for Gensei's grave, "Ah, the resting place of Gensei, a filial son!" It is said that Emyō, Gensei's successor as head of the temple, declined the honor on the grounds that it would conflict with Gensei's dying wishes, though in fact a marker with that inscription stands beside Gensei's grave today.

TRANSLATOR'S NOTE

MY REMARKS IN the Introduction may suggest that my only criterion for good poetry is that it be personal in tone. This is not quite the case. I believe I can appreciate the formal beauties of English poetry, and to a lesser extent those of poetry in Chinese and Japanese as well. But poetry that depends for its effectiveness principally upon musical effects or elaborate prosodic devices can seldom be translated with much success. And works that are outstanding for their adroit handling of conventional themes and images are difficult to appreciate unless one has a thorough knowledge of the conventions being drawn on, something that most readers of Asian poetry in translation can scarcely be expected to have. Thus, when selecting poems for translation, one naturally searches for those with interesting content, and finds them most often among works that deal with the writer's personal experiences.

Japanese *kanshi* writers, as one might expect, were seldom innovative in the medium. They looked to the Chinese to initiate new styles and forms, and then attempted to master the innovations. The aim of many *kanshi* writers, in a word, was simply to sound as authentically Chinese as possible.

From this it is obvious that if there is an element of originality, of unique Japaneseness, in *kanshi* poetry, it will most likely be found in those works that describe the writer's own life and experiences. Hence a second reason why I focus so assiduously on works of this kind, to the apparent neglect of poetry that deals in the creation of more impersonal and formally ordered worlds.

I might add here that Chinese and Japanese poetry has traditionally tended to be more occasional in nature, more closely tied to the time and place of composition, than most Western poetry. That is why so many Chinese and Japanese poems are prefaced by prose introductions describing the circumstances under which they were composed. The Western poet strives to express truths that transcend time and place. The Eastern poet is content if he can capture the particular truth that appeared to him at the moment of writing.

My translations of Gensei's poetry and prose in Chinese are based on the *Hōnchū Sōzanshū*, an edition of the *Sōzanshū* with head notes taken from a commentary on Gensei's work by his disciple Emyō, and the *Minobu no michi no ki* appended. The edition was published in 1911 by the Nichiren-shū zensho shuppankai and reprinted by Homman-ji, Kyoto, in 1977. In 1978 Homman-ji brought out a work in two volumes entitled *Sōzan shūi* which contains photographic reproductions of Gensei's other writings, such as religious works, poetry in Japanese, the collection of Chinese poems exchanged between himself and Ch'en Yüan-yün, etc. My translations of Gensei's Japanese poems are based on the *Shinshū Sōzan wakashū*, ed. Otouma Jitsuzō (Kyoto: Heiraku-ji shoten, 1927). Other works that I have found helpful in preparing this volume are listed below. Some of my Gensei translations have appeared earlier in *Zero* and *Ironwood*.

Aoyama Kason. *Fukakusa no Gensei*. Kyoto: Heiraku-ji shoten, 1909; reprinted 1936.
Koizumi Tōzō. *Gensei, Ryōkan, Guan*. Kyoto: Ritsumeikan shuppambu, 1936.

Komatsubara Tō. *Chin Gempin no kenkyū.* Tokyo: Yūzankaku, 1962.

Matsushita Tadashi. *Edo jidai no shifū shiron: Min, Shin no shiron to sono sesshu.* Tokyo: Meiji shoin, 1969.

Munemasa Isoo. "Gensei." *Bungaku gogaku* no. 58 (December 1970), pp. 69–78.

Munemasa Isoo. "Gensei—sono shutsuji," in his *Nihon kinsei bun'en no kenkyū.* Tokyo: Miraisha, 1977; pp. 9–33.

Otouma Jitsuzō. *Gensei shōnin.* Kyoto: Tōkō shorin, 1945.

Shimabara Yasuo. *Fakakusa Gensei-shū.* Tokyo: Koten bunko. 4 vols.
Vol. 1 (1977) contains Gensei's poems, diaries, and letters in Japanese. Vol. 2 (1978) discusses his biography and works. Vols. 3 and 4 (1977, 1978) contain three of his religious works, *Fusō in'itsu den, Honchō Hokke den,* and *Honchō tonshi.*

My selection includes works in the following Chinese poetic forms:

Old style (*ku-shih*). An early form, of unlimited length, usually employing a five-character (5-ch.) or seven-character (7-ch.) line. Even-numbered lines rhyme; the rhyme may change several times within a single poem.

Regulated verse (*lü-shih*). An 8-line form that uses a single rhyme throughout and requires verbal parallelism in the two middle couplets and tonal parallelism throughout.

Chüeh-chü. A form that closely resembles regulated verse but is only 4 lines in length.

P'ai-lü. A form that observes the rules of tonal parallelism but is unrestricted in length.

Tsa-t'i, or poem in mixed form. A poem that uses lines of varying or unusual length. All the above forms belong to the category of *shih* poetry.

Rhyme-prose (*fu*). A poetic form, usually narrative or descriptive, that uses lines of varying lengths, sometimes with a prose introduction or interludes. It often runs to considerable length.

POETRY

"The Dream Fades Above the Peak of Mount Hiei"

(5-ch. old style)

    I had a dream in which I hit on a couplet for a poem that went:

    One, one, one, three ones;
    thousand, thousand, thousand, so many thousands!

When I woke up I wrote it down. Dawn of the 24th day of the last month of the year, Manji era, the year with the cyclical sign *tsuchinoto-i* (1659).

    The dream fades above the peak of Mount Hiei;
    waking, I understand how to make the senses pure.
    In my dream I came on a couplet—
    the wording was lofty, the meaning new.
    And this I say to my friends:
    don't think you can call me a fool.
    Not even knowing that truth is a dream,
    how can you tell when a dream is true?

Facing the Lamp

(5-ch. old style)

Since I took sick I'm sleepless, restless,
facing the lamp, my back to the beautiful moon.
I lie reading Yüan Hung-tao,
pulling at my short hair in delight.
When the lamp dies I call for more oil
till the brightly glowing wick curls anew.
Since I took leave of the dusty world,
I've parted from all my old friends.
I wonder what bonds of karma, lamp,
keep us so unfailingly together?
When I was young I set off on the road to office,
on horseback starting out before dawn,
each morning scrambling into my clothes,
you hanging at my side so I wouldn't bump into things.
And then there were the boyhood games,
when we met at the Bon[1] festival:
gauze lanterns dangling from slanting poles—
I thought the more I had the happier I'd be.
A little older, I loved to read books;
ranks and stipends meant nothing to me.
Days I raced around, at night stole some leisure,
reading away alone, you always there to light me.
As a young man I decided to become a monk,
shut my door and delved for the truth.
But poor as I was, I had no need
to gather fireflies or snow.[2]

1. A Buddhist festival, held in summer, when the spirits of the dead are believed to visit their families. Lanterns are hung out to light their way, and there is feasting and dancing.

2. Reference to accounts of Chinese scholars who were too poor to buy oil for their lamps and had to read by the light of fireflies or moonlight reflected on the snow.

With you forever quiet by my side
I never noticed when the weariness crept into my bones.
I promise to keep your small flame burning,
never stopping for the rest of my life,
till you've changed into the bright light of wisdom,
for endless kalpas never going out.

"Fifteen Years You Kept Me Company"

(5-ch. old style)

I had a goosefoot walking stick that I had carried around with me for fifteen years. One evening the boy stepped on it and broke it. So I wrote a poem to console myself.

> Fifteen years you kept me company;
> I counted on you to prop up my strolls:
> humming, we wandered through the blossoms of the capital;
> travelers journeying under a barrier mountain moon.
> I'm not even forty yet
> but my bones and muscles are worn out already.
> Straw cape and hat I might dispense with,
> but my stick I can't do without for a moment.
> Who'd have thought—at the bottom of the empty stairs,
> one footfall and your life span was snapped in two!
> You're not a garment—you can't be mended,
> not a cord that can be retied.
> Shriveled up cane—one might have guessed your age,
> but what frail stuff you were made of!
> I look at this world of ours—
> everything that has a form fades away,
> "like the dew, like the lightning"—[1]
> so the Buddha preached, I've heard.
> Who could doubt the truth of it?
> Even heaven and earth have their time to end.

---

1. From the famous series of similes in the Diamond Sutra.

Luckily I've all this bamboo, green and burgeoning,
plenty to support my sinews and bones.
I'll cut it, fashion a new walking stick
to join me in guarding the late seasons of my life.

The Summit of Takagamine

(A steep hill northwest of Kyoto. See the prose piece on p. 89. 5-ch. old style.)

Green wall, like a palm turned edgewise,
no marks where shoe or walking stick might have passed.
Woodcutter's trail we pick up, then lose again;
clutching brambles, we hoist ourselves up to the roots of the clouds.
One step forward, then call to the others—
turning to look back, we nearly lose our nerve.
At last we reach the top of Takagamine—
what world are we in now?
Barely a foot away from the sky,
the red sun as though you could take it in your hand,
the world below so far away it's hard to make out,
hills and mountains like overturned bowls—
But these scenes have no ending;
why try to describe them with the senses?
If we want to hear the heavenly beings speaking
we must sit cross-legged, not say a word.

Looking Over the Marketplace

(5-ch. old style)

> I'm the kind of person who loves to read books;
> while there's still time, I search for a hundred authors.
> Though I've cut all my other ties with the world,
> this one I can't seem to put an end to,
> but always hoping to find some new book,
> I come to look over the Kyoto market.
> I'm like a thief intent on stealing someone's brocade,
> not even conscious of the noise and dust.[1]
> Among the bustle of these nine great avenues
> my mind is as clear and still as water,
> and everywhere I look my eyes spy treasures—
> why should it only be "the jewel in the garment"?[2]

1. According to the *Liu Tzu* or *Hsin lun*, a Chinese work of uncertain date, the law officials caught a thief trying to steal a piece of brocade in the midst of a crowded marketplace. Asked why he would attempt such an impossible feat, the thief replied, "I only saw the brocade, I didn't see the people." Gensei, speaking of his passion for books in a letter to a friend (*SZS* ch. 3, p. 63), remarks that in his previous incarnation he must have been a silverfish.

2. Reference to the parable in chapter 8 of the Lotus Sutra, which tells of a man who, unknown to himself, had a precious jewel hidden in his garment. The jewel is the Buddha nature.

"Sick So Often, I Hardly See My Old Friends"

(5-ch. old style)

Sekisai[1] came with his boy to visit my mountain temple. We apportioned rhymes and I got the rhyme *gai*.

> Sick so often, I hardly see my old friends;
> a year's gone by since we parted.
> Who'd have guessed, in this season of plum rains[2]
> you'd come to visit just as you promised?
> The mists have parted and I see the blue sky—
> what a pleasure, to chat and laugh together!
> And Seki my friend, you have this son,
> this son I'm truly awed by—
> still in boy's braids, he reads off what people write
> as swiftly as a boat shooting the rapids!
> Why should he merely carry on his father's business?
> For your sake, I want to see him do much greater things!
> A session of intoning, and now our rhymes are finished—
> long, drawn out, they put forth the piping of Heaven.[3]
> This damp mountain air has troubled me so long—
> now suddenly I feel as though I've shed my body;

---

1. Ukai Yukinobu (1616–1664), a Confucian scholar who at this time lived in Kyoto and supported himself by collating and punctuating Chinese texts and supplying marks for reading them in Japanese. He did much to spread a wider knowledge of Chinese literature.
2. The monsoon rainy season in June and early July.
3. Reference to *Chuang Tzu*, ch. 2.

my form remains in the realm of youth and age
but my spirit roams beyond the spheres.
Here in our poems, a thread of incense,
and together we enter the samadhi of Zen![4]

4. The preface to the *Kinshūdan* states, "Outside of poetry there is no Zen, outside of Zen there is no poetry." The *Kishūdan* is an anthology of Chinese poetry in *chüeh-chü* or quatrain form from the T'ang, Sung, and Yuan dynasties compiled by the Japanese Zen monk Ten'in Ryūtaku (1421–1500). The view that poetry and Zen are basically similar in nature derives from the *Ts'ang-lang shih-hua* or "Ts'ang-lang's Remarks on Poetry" by the Chinese critic Yen Yü (fl. 1180–1235).

Inscription for the What-Does-It-Matter Pavilion

(A country retreat at the foot of Mt. Arashi west of Kyoto. It was owned by a man known by the literary name Shūgenshi, whom Shimabara tentatively identifies with the poet Uchida Kagenori [d. 1670]. See Shimabara Yasuo, ed., *Fukakusa Gensei-shū* [Koten bunko], vol. 2, p. 176. 5-ch. old style.)

The Kameyama hill peers down in front,
Arashiyama curls around behind;
the Ōi River runs at the foot,
Mount Hiei rising on the right;
south of it, a range of tall peaks,
west the steep summit of Atago.
The True Breath congealed to give it form;
no hand of an immortal spirit shaped it.
But splendid spot though it is,
there's never been any fixed master.
Once the gate of thronging mysteries was opened,
each one found itself a room.
Expound no principles of truth here,
no frivolous discourses to spoil these quiet delights!
The flowing stream is our teacher of mindlessness,
the white clouds our unthinking friends.
If I were to try to describe it,
all I could do is give the lion's roar.[1]

1. The lion represents the Buddha, the roar his teachings.

"With the Long Rains We Couldn't Step Out the Gate"

(When two or more persons composed Chinese poems as a group, they customarily assigned each other the rhymes to be used in order to make the undertaking more challenging. 5-ch. old style.)

Apportioning rhymes with my disciples, I got the rhyme *sō*.

With the long rains we couldn't step out the gate;
dust has buried my goosefoot staff.
Now suddenly we've hit a bright clear day
and my ailing body takes on a whole new cast.
Older and younger call to each other,
taking hands along the mountain path.
Grass for a mat, we sit strung out in rows,
making the pines our shade, leaning on their snakey roots.
In one climb we've made it up so high,
looking down at the world is like peering at your palm.
River beds stretching hundreds of miles,
mountain peaks thousands of feet tall—
blowing out our breath, we stir the clouds and mist;
with a long shout, we startle the spirits and elves.
Wind from the sky never stops blowing,
and at times we hear the Buddha's clear voice.
How hard for the people of the world,
endless kalpas caught in its dusty coils,
never enjoying the truly fine pleasures,
tumbled head over heels by their thoughts and cares—
what day will they come to the green hills,
be our companions, join us in these strolls?

Relaxing at the Shōshin-an

(The Shōshin-an was the residence Gensei built for himself and his parents. Wu Kuo-lun is a 16th-century Chinese poet. 5-ch. regulated verse; two from a set of eight poems.)

Relaxing at the Shōshin-an, I wrote these for my amusement, using the rhyme *en* and letting the brush go any way it wanted. I followed the rhyme words used by Wu Kuo-lun in his "Visiting the Priest Lu."

I.
I share my quarters, take care of my mother,
half a layman, half a monk.
Since I remain in the dusty world,
let them call me a man of the Two Vehicles.[1]
I stroll in the Void, out of the burning house,
shut my door to protect the wind-blown lamp.[2]
Among the ten thousand affairs, there's nothing I seek—
perched on high, I'm like a sated hawk.

II.
Men of elegance hate the ways of the world,
the pure and lofty ones look down on a river monk.
But my goosefoot staff goes along with me walking,
and my firewood cart is fine for a ride.
On the platform is my zazen mat,
under the window, the lamp I read by.
And when I go out the gate and look around,
I see flocks of crows laughing at a country hawk.

1. "Two Vehicles" here represents a commitment and way of life less perfect than the One Vehicle taught in the Lotus Sutra.

2. The burning house symbolizes the temporal world, the wind-blown lamp the frailty of human life.

Following the Rhymes of a Poem by Giō

(Giō was Gensei's chief disciple at this time; see p. 93. 5-ch. regulated verse.)

The ten thousand things offer patterns enough,
heaven and earth like one big loom:
in the dark wood blossoms unfold of themselves,
above the broad meadow, birds idly soar.
Ripples pile up—the water's folding its mat;
clouds part—the mountain doffing its robe.
This mist and haze—we'll make them our friends,
long as we can, stay clear of the dusty world.

Troubled by Rain

(5-ch. regulated verse)

> Dragon kings send down axle-size shafts of rain—
> from the porch I watch the paddies forming.
> My ears ring with the drip that falls from the paulownias,
> eyes water in smoke from the damp firewood.
> I poke my pillow, turning it over a thousand times,
> shift my bed—how many moves have I made?
> Suppose I do live in Yüan Hsien's hovel—[1]
> I can still enjoy what Heaven gives me.

1. *Chuang Tzu* ch. 28 gives a graphic description of the shoddy two-room hut occupied by Yüan Hsien, a disciple of Confucius known for his indifference to poverty.

Visiting Ise Temple, Describing What I See

(5-ch. regulated verse)

    Morning sun once more slants its rays,
    the green of mountain peaks already gone yellow.
    Mount Ikoma emerges from a passing shower,
    Lion Cave still stashed away in cloud.
    Beyond the Yodo, the Amano in the distance,
    fields stretching in a long sweep to Kin'ya.
    I've heard of the Nagisa Lodge of long ago—
    its snow of cherries, who do they bloom for now?[1]

1. Ise Temple is in Takatsuki, on the west bank of the Yodo. Mount Ikoma runs down the east side of the river. Lion Cave is the site of a famous temple of that name on a northern peak of Ikoma. The Amano is a tributary of the Yodo. Kin'ya or "forbidden fields" is an area at the foot of Ikoma that was an imperial hunting preserve in Heian times. The Nagisa Lodge was nearby, at a place now called, because of the lodge, Gotenyama; it was used by Emperor Montoku and later his eldest son, Prince Koretaka. The last line refers to a famous cherry-viewing party held there by Prince Koretaka and described in *Ise monogatari*, sec. 82. See Helen Craig McCullough, tr., *Tales of Ise* (Tokyo: University of Tokyo Press, 1968), pp. 124–26.

Written in the Boat Going Home from Takatsuki

(5-ch. regulated verse)

Up at dawn in Takatsuki,
a little boat for the journey home:
Mount Ikoma hidden, veiled in rain,
Dove Peak, waves borne on it, flowing away.
The monk lean—a crane peering into the water;
people far off—birds standing on the shoals.
And that stupid boy of mine has to ruin it all,
sound asleep, snoring his ragged snores!

Evening View from Grass Hill

(5-ch. regulated verse)

In love with mountains, I go out my gate,
then lay aside the staff, rest on a pine root.
Autumn rivers border the broad fields,
twilight haze parts me from the distant village.
As dew rises, the edges of the grove whiten;
stars come out and tree tops grow blacker.
I can tell I've been sitting here a long time—
the dark moss already bears my print.

Mourning for the Wife of Kada Nobuaki: Preface and Poem

(The Kada family were Shinto priests of the Inari Shrine in Fushimi, and were also experts in Japanese poetry. Gensei visited the shrine often, wrote poems in Chinese and Japanese describing it and his relations with the family [see p. 106], and received criticisms of his Japanese poems. Kada Nobuaki was the father of the famous poet and scholar of Japanese literature, Kada no Azumamaro [1669–1736]. 5-ch. regulated verse.)

The recluse of Lone Hill had no wife or children, but referred to the plum blossoms as his "wife" and the cranes as his "children."[1] I have no wife or children either. I make the bright autumn moon my wife and the blossoms and bamboo my children. Perhaps this is something like having the joy of the Dharma for a wife and pity and goodness for your children.[2] In the stillness of the autumn night there is no one in my bed—I am alone, looking at the moon, and so full of delight I don't even realize it when the east is about to brighten. This year too the second month of autumn is drawing to a close. Rain has beaten down the blossoms and bamboo, and the full moon of autumn too has gone. In vain I look up at the vast sky and sigh that Hsün Feng-ch'ien will never see his lovely one again.[3]

Mr. Kada of the nearby shrine has recently lost his wife. If we cannot bear to part even from such unfeeling things as the moon and the flowers, how much greater is the grief

---

1. Lin Pu (967–1028), an eccentric Chinese poet who lived at Lone Hill on West Lake near Hangchow.

2. Reference to the Vimalakirti Sutra, ch. 8, the words of Vimalakirti, "The joy of the Dharma I make my wife, the mind of pity and compassion is my daughter."

3. Hsün Feng-ch'ien, described in *Shih-shuo hsin-yü* sec. 35 and commentary, had a beautiful wife whom he loved dearly and nursed in sickness. When she died, he lamented that he would "never see his lovely one again."

that wounds us at a time like this! So in the end I wrote a poem in regulated verse to take the place of a tub-pounding song.[4] My hope is that, by humming it over softly, you may lessen your sorrow a little.

> Flowers and moon—you parted from these unfeeling things;
> how much bitterer now as you lie in bed alone!
> In her room, dust shrouds her mirror;
> beneath the trees, bamboo buries her fragrance.
> Evening rain—a thousand streams of tears;
> dawn clouds—ten thousand knots in the heart.
> Perhaps it's time for a tub-pounding song—
> who stays for long in this drifting world of ours?

4. Reference to the song that Chuang Tzu sang when his wife died. *Chuang Tzu* ch. 18.

Green Shade

(5-ch. regulated verse)

Here among the dense wooded hills,
a single hut cut off from ten thousand ties.
The red dust of the world never reaches it,
but the white sun lingers, forgetting to move on.
The moon comes, battling its way before the wind,
dew drips down in the wake of rain.
Green, green—no color but this,
as though I were dwelling in the Tushita Heaven![1]

1. Fourth of the six heavens in the world of desire, its characteristic color is green.

"Rain Cleared, My Ailment Seems a Bit Better"

(5-ch. regulated verse)

1663, 6th month, 9th day. I took my mother for an outing to Valley Mouth.

Rain cleared, my ailment seems a bit better—
I go with my mother on an outing.
We float melons on the water to wake ourselves from
    the burning heat,
brew tea to wash away delusions.
Bamboos struggle, bowing before the clear breeze;
the blinds sway, rippling with the shallow stream.
We shake out our robes in this secluded valley
and summer's ninety days become the three months of
    fall!

Thoughts in a Famine Year

(5-ch. regulated verse)

Eighth month and still it barely rains—
they dig channels to set the waterwheels turning.
Desperate to get by, people abandon their children;
the woods so lean the bamboos put out blossoms.[1]
Ragged grass pokes up through the cracked earth,
crazed insects get into the teeth of the dogs.
I'm astounded that we should be so lucky—
fragrant rice and the aroma of tea!

1. Most species of bamboo bloom only at rare intervals, after which the plants wither. Here the blooming is apparently thought to be related to the drought.

Outing to the Hachiman Shrine of Kanju-ji

(Kanju-ji, also called Kajū-ji, is a Shingon temple in Yamashina, just over the hill from Gensei's temple. Hachiman is the deified form of the ancient ruler Emperor Ōjin who, according to legend, was transformed into a golden falcon. The white dove is the sacred messenger of Hachiman. At this time, most Buddhist temples had Shinto shrines attached to them. The Hachiman Shrine is on a hillside just south of Kanju-ji. 5-ch. *p'ai-lü*.)

    Winter so warm, it's like a spring scene:
    the boys in hand, I start up the mountain slopes.
    Shrine of an immortal, its jade-green doors locked,
    a monk's cell, the stone portal closed:
    I rest on a rock, take off my hat,
    scoop from the spring with my hands, shake out my robe.
    Golden falcon, where are your transformations?
    White doves fly through these woods.
    We chanced along with the drifting clouds;
    now we follow the flowing stream home.
    The gods, they say, praise the empty hills,
    but they must resent it when visitors are so few!

Distant View from Grass Hill

(7-ch. regulated verse)

> My one puny hut leads right off to the slopes,
> but few visitors hike up to the top of Grass Hill.
> Cows wandering here and there look almost like flocks of crows;
> herons heading home to roost in the village you'd take for darting butterflies.
> Clouds break, and beyond the treetops a lone pagoda rises;[1]
> where wind parts the reed leaves, the single sail of a homecoming boat.
> These scenes have their limits but my mind has none;
> still seated on a pine root, I see off the evening sun.

1. Probably the tall five-story pagoda of Tō-ji Temple near the southern edge of Kyoto, built in 1644 and until recent years the tallest structure in the city.

Troubled with Boils

(7-ch. regulated verse)

> Swellings boil up on my body like fires raging;
> why must these hundred ailments afflict me one after another?
> I can barely fold my legs to sit in dragon-coil position;
> my right side won't let me sleep in the lion's rest.[1]
> These peaks and pits in my skin, as though stones were wrapped in it;
> around my waist, these up and downs, like mountain ranges piled up.
> In pain and grief I pass my days, but why should I resent it?
> These "swelling tumors, protruding wens" are all the work of Heaven.[2]

1. "Dragon-coil" is the cross-legged position used in Buddhist meditation; "lion's rest" is the position in which the Buddha died, lying on his right side.

2. *Chuang Tzu* ch. 6; "They look upon life as a swelling tumor, a protruding wen, and upon death as the draining of a sore or the bursting of a boil."

Narcissus Flowers: Preface and Poems

(Third from a set of five 5 ch. *chüeh-chü*)

At the end of the first month of spring, I went to Takatsuki to undergo treatment for my illness. Except for myself and the boy with me, there were no other members of the clergy around; everywhere I looked I saw only plain-robed laymen and laywomen. I was feeling rather dejected in such surroundings, and all the acupuncture and medicine and moxa-burning had me in a muddle. I was quite joyless until by chance I had the luck to come on several stalks of narcissus in bloom. Their immortal airs[1] and doctrinal bones suddenly showed me how to break free from these entanglements of the dusty world. I was no longer aware that the moxa was burning on my skin, and I let my mouth shape these little poems.

> White jacket like a feathered immortal,
> yellow face resembling an old Buddha:
> when causes act upon the Absolute,
> in the midst of the dust we see things like this!

1. The narcissus is known in Chinese and Japanese by a name that means "water immortal."

Letting the Brush Write Anything It Wants

(Three from a set of five 5-ch. *chüeh-chü*)

I.
My mind contemplates the Dharma of No Birth,
my mouth intones rhymeless poems,
my mother's old and I'm sick most of the time—
if I weren't happy, I'd be a fool for sure.

II.
I strain for wisdom, get stupider than ever,
work at cleverness only to become more clumsy.
What I really love are these children's songs—
they have no tune, and yet they have a tune.

III.
Spring waters, patterned in pointless beauty,
summer clouds making strange peaks of their own—
if you'll just set aside your theories,
we can begin to talk about poetry.

Bamboo Leaf Hut: Preface and Poems

(Three from a set of ten 5-ch. *chüeh-chü*)

Bamboo Leaf Hill is another name for Grass Hill. It's been several years since I rigged a shelter out of yellow thatch and began living here. Recently I decided I would like to build another little building and name it Bamboo Leaf Hut. I thought I could use it now and then to sit in meditation or march around the room, read and recite scriptures or sing away to myself. But it has yet to be built.

The late summer heat in the seventh month this year is so fierce that I've suspended my teaching and research. The hills are quiet, the days long, and all day I stroll back and forth under the tall bamboo. The leaves seem to hold in the breeze and you can almost scoop up the clear cool air with your hands. It's not the kind of elegant pastime you can describe very well in words, but I put down whatever came to mind and made these ten poems in five-character form on the Bamboo Leaf Hut.

I.
In front of the roof, bamboo leaves dangling;
behind the roof, bamboo leaves beyond;
above the roof, bamboo leaves sheltering;
in the middle, a journeyor in love with bamboo.

II.
Body light as bamboo leaves,
bamboo leaves like little boats
drifting through the great emptiness,
following the wind, floating free.

III.
Inside its joints, the hollow of emptiness;
on the leaves, the color of form,[1]
form and emptiness basically one,
and I hide myself in their midst.

1. Heart Sutra: "Form is none other than emptiness, emptiness is none other than form."

Giō Boils Tea

(7-ch. *chüeh-chü*)

> With red leaves left after frost that you gathered under the trees
> you brew tea, call me in—a most generous thought!
> We sit here not speaking—the mountain window is still,
> but pine winds from ten thousand peaks stir in the kettle.[1]

1. The last line alludes to a poem by the Chinese Zen monk Chieh-shih Chih-p'eng (mid-13th century) entitled "Simmering Tea on Mount Hui" from the anthology *Chiang-hu feng-yüeh-chi*:

> In an earthen jar at break of day I dip clean cold water,
> shift it to the stone kettle, boil it on a broken slab.
> Pine winds from ten thousand peaks I offer in one sip,
> then gather my sleeves together, walk by the waterside.

Happy at Giō's Return

(7-ch. *chüeh-chü*)

After we parted, I stood gazing east and west;
you're back, one laugh and my worries turn to air.
These chapters of travel diary—their marvelous phrases
set me right down in the dark mountain valley mists!

Coming Home Late from Kyoto

(7-ch. *chüeh-chü*)

Sundown I gaze at cloudy hills that rise beyond the city,
crowds and crowds of palanquins, a long road ahead.
Chasing profit, galloping after fame—no concern of mine.
Riding the moonlight, I fly over Gojō Bridge.

The Grave of Ears

(A mound in the grounds of Hōkō-ji Temple in Kyoto containing the ears and noses of Chinese and Koreans killed in Toyotomi Hideyoshi's infamous campaign against Korea in 1592–98. The ears and noses were pickled and sent back to Japan as war trophies. 7-ch. *chüeh-chü*.)

> They took the pickles, brought them back, built this grave mound here:
> pity those who parted from loving parents ten thousand miles away.
> A poem in Japanese would mean little to foreign ears—
> I struggle to fashion a Chinese poem to comfort these wandering souls.

Following the Rhymes of Giō's Poem Urging Me to Drink Tea: Preface and Poem

(7-ch. *chüeh-chü*)

I have been in mourning for my father and more than usually troubled by sickness. In addition, the spring rains come pouring down incessantly, the thatch leaks, the beams get damp—it's almost too gloomy and depressing to bear. And then Giō composed this poem in *chüeh-chü* form urging me to drink some tea. I was sure his intention was to bring me some relief from the sorrow of mourning and sickness and so I pushed my pillow aside, read the poem, and then got up and drank some tea. Now I am following his rhymes in an attempt to convey something of my thoughts, inconsequential as they are. Ah! Although my initial grief and desolation may have come to an end, I do not feel capable of composing a proper poem. But they say that those who are suffering the pain of mourning needn't meet all the demands of etiquette, so I hope you will be lenient with me.

> Wind buffets the thatched roof, rain soaks my house—
> can I bear this mourning on top of lifetime ills?
> They say no liquids enter the mouth of a filial son—[1]
> shameful, that I should have the heart to savor this tea!

1. According to *Li chi*, *T'an Kung* pt. 1, Tseng Tzu declared that when he was in mourning for a parent, he took no liquid for seven days. The *Li chi* itself, however, recommends only three days of such abstinence. Gensei's father died in the 12th month of Manji 1st year, which would have fallen in early 1658, at the age of 86.

Incense Stick
(7-ch. *chüeh-chü*)

    Thread from its tip a tangled strand, white clouds fragrant,
    rising in a hundred shifting shapes, never constant for a moment;
    deep in good conversation, a foot-long stick seems short,
    but when you're weary of doing zazen, even one inch is too long![1]

1. The incense stick is used to time the duration of a period of zazen or Buddhist style meditation.

Evening Stroll

(7-ch. *chüeh-chü*)

Evening stroll, enjoying the clear weather, my stick for companion,
deep in the thick grove, content to go east or west;
in particular I love these plants that have no names,
the kind never found in the poet's list of topics.

"The Boy Emperor Begins His Ten Thousand Year Reign"

(7-ch. *chüeh-chü*)

In the year with the cyclical sign *mizunoto-u* (1663), the first month of summer, the twenty-seventh day, a new emperor ascended the throne.[1] I happened to be in Kyoto. It rained in the morning, and afterward the sky was overcast and the day quiet. I went to bed, and as soon as I awoke, I got up, laughed to myself and wrote this:

> The boy emperor begins his ten thousand year reign;
> one shower of rain drenches down, filling all the nine avenues.
> Today Ch'en T'uan would think it right to give a big laugh—
> times are peaceful, the kind to insure you lots of sound sleep![2]

1. Emperor Reigen, the son of Emperor Gomizunoo, who succeeded his older brother Emperor Gosaii at the age of nine and reigned until 1687.

2. Ch'en T'uan was a philosopher of the early Sung period. According to *Lieh-hsien ch'üan-chuan* ch. 7, he was in the habit of shutting his gate and sleeping for several months at a time. During the Hsien-te era (954–60) of Emperor Shih-tsung of the Later Chou, a woodcutter spied something at the foot of a mountain that looked like an abandoned corpse covered with dust, but when he got closer, he saw that it was Mr. Ch'en. After some time, Ch'en got up and said, "I was sleeping so soundly—why'd you have to bother me!" Later, when he heard that Emperor T'ai-tsu, founder of the Sung dynasty, had ascended the throne, he clapped his hands, gave a big laugh and said, "From now on, the world will be at peace!"

Matching the Poem on Wisdom Gruel: Preface and Poem

(7-ch. *chüeh-chü*)

In our temple, there was a little boy who, when he was no more than six years old, used to wait on my elderly parents. He was always watching what the monks did and wishing he could be one of them, and quite on his own he gave up eating meat and strong flavored foods for three or four years. My mother was very fond of him and promised him that he could become a monk.

One day he came to my room, made a very formal bow, and said, "I want to be a monk. I would like to be given a monk's name." His name as a child was Ko or Tiger, and so I decided we should call him Kosai. He was very pleased and from then on used that as his name.

Recently he has been studying the Lotus Sutra and has now completed his studies. It's a custom with us that on the day when someone completes his study of the Lotus Sutra, we always cook a kind of rice gruel with red beans that we call "wisdom gruel." My mother accordingly made the gruel and served it to everyone in our temple group. Tōmoku, a Zen monk from Hanazono, just happened to come along and join us, and he composed a verse to celebrate the occasion. I recklessly chimed in with the following sequel.

The gruel of sweet dew fills your bowl:
taste it and you'll know that it is ghee.

Once you gain the one thousand two hundred blessings of the tongue,
then bitter, acid, salty, sour will forever seem the same.[1]

1. Sweet dew in Indian legend is the nectar of immortality; ghee, the most delicious of beverages, is used in Buddhism as a symbol of the highest truth. According to chapter 19 of the Lotus Sutra, one who reads and recites the sutra will receive "one thousand two hundred blessings of the tongue" by which all flavors will be rendered delicious.

Hut: Preface and Poem

(The poem is in *tsa-t'i* or mixed form. The language recalls the ancient Chinese folksongs in the *Book of Odes*.)

In my hut I was thinking of my friend. My friend had not come to see me for a long time, and because I was ill I couldn't go to pay a visit. In longing, I wrote this poem.

I waited for you in my hut, I did—
silent, silent, feeling little joy,
but today again the sun is setting.

I waited for you by the gate, I did—
silent, silent, not speaking a word,
but today again twilight's coming on.

I waited for you along the road, I did—
silent, silent, walking alone,
but today again the darkness begins to fall.

To Send Off My Elder Yüan-yün [1]

(One of a set of ten poems in *tsa-t'i* or mixed form.)

    Since that chance encounter at Owari Castle,
    already now four years have passed.
    This year we meet in Kyoto—
    such coming and going must wear out an old man's staff!
    Lively conversation, not a touch of the crass;
    we forget each other like two old fools.
    You can speak the Japanese language
    but your native sounds remain in your tongue.
    Thanks to long practice, I get nine-tenths of what you say,
    but bystanders can't make out a word.

1. The Chinese emigré Ch'en Yüan-yün, whom Gensei met at Nagoya in Owari in 1659. At this time Ch'en was 76 and Gensei 39. When Hara Nensai (1774–1820) compiled a biography of Ch'en Yüan-yün for his *Sentetsu Sōdan* or "Collected Anecdotes on Former Philosophers," he quoted the last four lines of this poem.

Four Ceremonies of a Mountain Home: Preface and Poems

(tsa-t'i)

My fellow monk Shōko has written a poem entitled "Mountain Home" that describes just what it's like to live in the mountains—vivid and free in expression, truly admirable. I have accordingly used the same rhyme words to make these poems on Four Ceremonies of a Mountain Home.

I.
Mountain home walking,
you don't step on dust,
seldom meet anyone—
who's ashamed to be poor?
Tired? then rest—
what do you need a mat for?
Forget about the form
and the shadow will disappear.

II.
Mountain home living,
no dust in an aeon.
You love how long the days are,
never notice you're poor.
Where moss is green,
better than embroidered mats.
Stand very still here
and your tracks will disappear.

III.
Mountain home sitting,
no dust to brush away,

bamboo to lean against—
just right when you're honestly poor.
I've a *nishidan* here—
that'll do for a mat.[1]
Even without these meditations
the world of form will disappear.

IV.
Mountain home sleeping,
no dreams of dust.
Three robes are plenty—[2]
who says I'm poor?
One for my pillow,
one to serve as mat,
and at the thunder of my snoring
Heaven and Earth disappear.

1. Sanskrit *nishīdana*, a cloth used for sitting, thrown over the shoulder when not in use.
2. *Sanne*, the three robes that a monk is permitted to own.

Autumn, a Visit to the Byōdō-in

(The Byōdō-in, a temple in Uji south of Kyoto, was built in 1052 and in Gensei's time appears to have been in a state of considerable neglect. Situated beside the Uji River, it fronts on a pond, called in the poem "merit-giving" because of the charitable nature of Buddhist intitutions. The sutra inscription on the panel on the south wall was formerly believed to be from the hand of Minamoto no Shumbō, though now it is generally attributed to Fujiwara no Kaneyuki. The central image is a gilded statue of the Buddha Amida by the famous sculptor Jōchō [d. 1057]. Minamoto no Takakuni [1004–1077], better known by the title Uji Dainagon, had a summer retreat near the temple called Nansen-in or Cloister of the Southern Springs. 7-ch. regulated verse, 1665.)[1]

Forest trees stripped in autumn, an ancient Buddhist temple,
where mists from the waters are deepest, dark even in day time.
The magnificent hall weathered, red and green paint peeled off;
the pond meant to bring merit gone dry, only lotuses left.
On the silver-leafed panel still remaining, Shumbō's writing;
the golden countenance untouched by time, Jōchō's handiwork.
The old Cloister of the Southern Springs—where is it now?
Not a soul passing this way, evening winds are chill.

1. From here on the poems are taken from the latter part of the *Sōzanshū*, which is arranged chronologically, so it is possible to date them.

Uji, Written on the Spur of the Moment

(7-ch. *chüeh-chü*, 1665)

I.
Ten thousand mile long river, ten thousand mile waves—
how many times have they hummed and broken off, singing the poet's song?[1]
Coming, going, coming, going, over the Uji bridge,
while I stand in the autumn wind, full of so many thoughts.

II.
All day in mountain mist and mountain haze
quietly I watch the autumn water, face the autumn sky.
Evening comes and the morning fog suddenly turns to rain:
add to the scene a single boat, old man in straw cape and hat.

1. The poem in the Man'yōshū (no. 264) by Kakinomoto no Hitomaro (c. 700) entitled "On the way from the province of Ōmi to the capital, by the Uji River":

> In the Uji, river of
> eighty warrior clans,
> the waves that hover
> around the fish weir pilings—
> no one knows where they go

On the Road to Sumiyoshi [1]

(5-ch. regulated verse, 1665)

> Violent rains have raised the level of the river;
> the new clear spell summons ocean breezes.
> A thousand mountains beyond the pine trees,
> a single road through the grass and weeds:
> the boy offers me the green of spring tea,
> the groom dispenses the red of autumn fruit.
> Muddy paths, and our trip not over yet—
> where in the world is the Dragon King's palace?

1. A famous Shinto shrine on the ocean south of Osaka dedicated to the patron deity of seafarers. According to legend, the Dragon King has his palace at the bottom of the sea.

Miscellaneous Songs from a Hot Spring

(Composed at Arima hot spring, where Gensei had gone for his health in the autumn of 1665. Two from a set of ten poems in 5-ch. regulated verse.)

I.
I live quietly with the other temple monks,
get up at dawn to chant *Namu*.
The valley stream transcends clamor and stillness,
mountain clouds know nothing of being or nonbeing.
Room half-a-span wide, empty enough to hang a bell in;
gruel in a gourd bowl that might be left dangling.[1]
And since I came here, what have I done?
"Bathed in the Yi, enjoyed the breeze in the rain altars."[2]

II.
Twilight scene in a hot-spring temple,
autumn wind, a mountain where leaves flutter down:
people hurry along with the valley stream,
birds go home in company with the white clouds.
Monks' quarters in the middle of the dusty town,
laymen's houses among the emerald of the woods.[3]
All day long on the bridge above the ravine
the green peaks face me in silence.

1. Someone, feeling sorry for the recluse Hsü Yu because he had to drink water from his hands, gave him a gourd dipper. But after using it once, Hsü Yu hung it on a tree and went off, leaving it to clatter in the wind.

2. From the famous passage in *Analects* XI, 25, in which one of Confucius' disciples describes his idea of an ideal outing.

3. During the middle ages, Buddhist monks established temples in Arima that served as inns for persons wishing to take the baths; Gensei was staying at one such temple. Here he remarks that, contrary to the situation in ordinary towns, in Arima the temples are located in the center of town and the homes of the ordinary citizens are on the surrounding hills.

Impromptu

(7-ch. *chüeh-chü*, 1665)

> I love this poor, rundown, silent village,
> my three robes, assorted gear, zazen platform.
> Outside these, what joys might a humble man have?
> A ninety-year-old parent still here with me!

Visiting the Heiraku-an

(The Heiraku-an was a small building in the grounds of the temple built by the bookseller Murakami Motonobu in memory of his parents. Two from a set of seven 5-ch. *chüeh-chü*, 1666.)

I.
I sit alone in my dark valley,
and who can I speak my mind to?
Twiddling a brush, I write down thoughts, that's all—
how could my poems be called poems?

II.
I myself laugh at how clumsy my poems are,
though my mind teems with the great odes of antiquity.
Only the mountain birds consent to join in,
voices here and there from the cloudy trees.

Valley Mouth: Preface and Poem

(Tsa-t'i, 1666)

In Mist Valley there is a place called Taniguchi or Valley Mouth, a lonely little hamlet with a stream running through it and hills ranged all around. There is a country-style teahouse built right over the stream and travelers coming and going in front of it. An old man and woman wait on customers; they have just one son. They are simple and unpretentious, like the people of old times. They make tea to pay for their living, and don't seem to have any particular wants. I'm very fond of them and from time to time go to spend some leisure there. My song says:

> Valley Mouth stream, Valley Mouth hills,
> a teahouse simple and countrified,
> people old-fashioned, unhurried.
> I love the faraway feeling,
> come to relax a while and always forget to go home.
> Someone said to me,
> "Hills and streams may be delightful,
> but it's not really secluded—I'd hate those passers-by!
> An old country fellow may be engaging,
> but I'd hate a man who knew nothing of words or writing!"
> I replied,
> "You've no taste at all, have you!
> How can passers-by spoil your objective?
> You can be among them and still have thoughts of your own.

Haven't you ever heard of the old man called Semi-
    maru?[1]
The old country fellow doesn't understand words or
    writing,
but those with no writing are the true ancients,
and those with no words are the truly leisured.
We might call him the grandfather of the untaught.
If I'm not to be this man's follower,
who should I take for my companion?

---

1. A semi-legendary blind poet and musician of the Heian period who lived at the barrier at Ōsaka or Meeting Slope on the main highway going east from Kyoto. Gensei is thinking in particular of Semimaru's famous poem:

> This is the spot—
> where those going, those returning
> take their leave,
> those who know each other, those who don't,
> the barrier at Meeting Slope

Written on Getting Up from a Nap

(7-ch. *chüeh-chü*, 1666)

> Steamy rain drizzling down, too lazy to read a book;
> by the north window, a pleasant nap, coarse matting for company:
> I've taken sick, but still I go on teaching lessons—
> I'd be ashamed to have my boys take after Tsai Yü![1]

1. Disciple of Confucius who was scolded by the master for sleeping in the daytime.

Climbing Up to Daigo-ji [1] *To View the Moon: Preface and Poems*

(One from a set of five 5-ch. regulated verse poems, 1666.)

On the evening before the full moon of the second month of autumn, I climbed up to Daigo-ji and spent the night at South Glen. The spot is a very isolated one, lonely and still. Outside of the brook in the glen, there's nothing else that makes a sound. Truly it is a place for carrying out esoteric religious practices.

The overseer of the lodge said to me, "This is the place where the Vinaya Master Ichijō lived long ago. According to what has been reported, he was the fifth son of Emperor Daigo and had the title Tōin no Zasu.[2] He devoted himself with great diligence to difficult religious practices and used to pound all his own incense. The pestle he used is still preserved here."

The fifth son of Emperor Daigo, I thought to myself, was Imperial Prince Jōmyō. But I never knew that later in life he became a monk. Presently the moon appeared from among the rocks on the peak, now clouding over, now shin-

---

1. Daigo-ji is a famous center of Shingon or Esoteric Buddhism in Yamashina east of Kyoto. It is in two parts, Shimo Daigo or "Lower Daigo," a cluster of temple buildings at the foot of the mountain, with a second group, known as Kami Daigo or "Upper Daigo," on top of the mountain. Gensei spent the night at Upper Daigo, which is reached by a strenuous climb up a steep path. In the fifth poem in the series, he mentions that he wrote a letter home the following day and sent it off with a servant, adding, "My servant is rather dense, so I told him again and again, 'Don't mention I spent the night on this high peak!'" He was evidently worried about what his mother would think of such an expedition.

2. Someone has his facts mixed up. Ichijō lived 880 to 945 and his family background is unknown. Emperor Daigo lived 885 to 930.

ing clear again. One thing after another caught my attention in this secluded setting, and it was a long time before I got to sleep.

> I didn't wait till it was ten parts full,
> but since autumn's here, climbed to the upper temple:
> the peak so high, the moon shines with a special brilliance,
> the mountain so still I hear the long drawn out sound of dripping water.
> Brewed in a saucer, Sonshi's tea;
> burned in a censer, the Zasu's incense.[3]
> Who knows that I'm in this dark glen,
> sitting in a silent room, face to the moon?

3. Sonshi Shimitsu, a monk of Daigo-ji, used to read all night, keeping a saucer of tea by his side in case he got sleepy. See *Genkō shakusho* ch. 4, biography of Daigo Shōhō.

Chestnuts

(7-ch. *chüeh-chü*, 1666)

> Among the leaves, cluster on cluster, green-spined porcupines,
> jolting each other in the west wind, not yet willing to drop:
> come the frost, they'll open their mouths, give an engaging smile,
> and then we'll see the monkeys crowding our mountain garden!

Following Shih-te's Rhymes

(A set of poems in 5-ch. old style that follow the rhyme words of poems attributed to Shih-te [Jittoku] or The Foundling, a Chinese recluse-poet associated with Han-shan or the Master of Cold Mountain. [See my *Cold Mountain: 100 Poems by the T'ang Poet Han-shan* (New York: Columbia University Press, 1970).] Though Gensei employs the rhyme words of Shih-te's poems, he does not usually imitate their content. The selection represents the 1st, 9th, 13th, 16th, 47th and 54th poems in the series. The series was published separately under the title *Seibon shōwa* or "Matching Poems of a Holy Man and a Plain Man." The preface to the series is translated on p. 103.)

I.
What a pain—these people with so much wisdom!
Even the Buddhas have trouble converting them.
They keep the sutra pages turning, but never turn their mind;
ten thousand volumes cram their bookshelves—all for nothing!
They've sunk into the pit of fame and profit,
day and night a prey to disquiet and fear.
Their hearts in the end care nothing for sincerity
but moment by moment plot some clever scheme.

II.
My poems—of course they're not poems;
and please don't call them hymns either!
I blurt out whatever's on my foot-square mind,
no need for fancy polishing or trimming.
If I want to use them to teach my boys,
the words have to be simple and easy.
I don't write them for the sake of poetry,
only for the sake of the "one big affair."[1]

---

1. *Ichidaiji*, the "one big affair" that the Buddhas appear in the world to tend to, i.e., the bringing of all beings to enlightenment. For purposes of comparison, I add here a translation of the corresponding poem by Shih-

III.
Monks don't know how to be monks,
busily busily pursuing worldly affairs:
they read sutras but are strangers to quiet meditation,
recite the commandments—then do as they please!
Minds clinging to marks of distinction,
their mouths discourse on all-encompassing truth.
The world's full of stupid and benighted people,
and in dense droves they flock around you!

IV.
You go by the name of Foundling,
I call myself Son of the Mystic Law,
both of us followers of the Buddha,
the two of us brothers, holy man and plain.
A thousand years after, I echo your hymns,
each of us speaking out his thoughts.
I clap my hands, at times laugh out loud—
clouds scatter, the moon shines clear.

V.
Why practice quiet sitting?
So you can really get a look at your original mind.
You look at it coming, look at it going,
and then you know you're the original man.
This latter age has no deep faith,
no one practices the direct road to understanding.

---

te; as one may see, this is a case where Gensei followed the rhymes of Shih-te's poem but not the sense.

> My poems—they're poems too;
> some people even call them hymns.
> Poems and hymns are on the whole alike—
> when you read them you've got to go at it with care,
> slowly, slowly, carefully probing—
> don't rashly assume its all simple and easy.
> Use poems to learn how to practice the Way—
> then you'll find it a hugely laughable affair!

All they do is flap three inches of tongue
and lose themselves in the muddle of the mind.

VI.
Half my life sitting by rocks and fountains,
my study cold, seldom the steam of tea:
white clouds emerge from the stillness,
in the valley stream the water runs clear.
I had no good karma to begin with,
so I was born into this muddy age.
Yet I know there's some past blessing,
for I've escaped the layman's life, shut my gate among
    clouds.
Alms bowl in hand, I roam the village streets;
grasping my staff, I climb the wooded peaks.
Sometimes I drift in the moonlight by Uji Bridge,
an empty boat free to follow the purls and eddies.
I never go against what the mind desires—
all this time I've been spared the din of the capital!

Visiting the Old Family Home at Kujō; Following Kan'yo's Rhymes

(The house where Gensei's parents lived before he was born and where he often visited in his youth. At this time it was occupied by Suekazu, a son of the Kawamoto family whom Gensei's father had adopted as an heir to carry on the Kujō branch of the family, since his eldest son was in the service of the Ii family and his younger sons had died or become monks. Kan'yo was a Zen monk Gensei took along as a guest on his visit. 5-ch. old style, 1667).

Over a month since the new year began—
the days flow by like water.
Moved by the times, recalling "those mulberries,"[1]
I took my friend in hand, set off for the place where my
    parents lived.
Tall trees just as in the past—
with reverence I go in among the old catalpas.
The barefoot servant, old now, tends the gate;
yellow warblers sing unceasingly.
Sorrows press in on me
as I turn my head, gaze at those around.
The rickety house still holds up,
    though hardly to be counted on to keep out wind and
    rain.
My father's death—like something I dreamed last night;
these passing phantoms make the years fly even faster.
Even if former times could come again,
we're better served by our present joy.
Not my father alone I recall—
distant ancestors too I pay respects to here.

---

1. Reference to *Book of Odes*, Mao no. 197, "Those mulberries and catalpas [of one's old home],/ one must think of them with reverence."

The world has seen its shifts and upheavals;
one hates the purple for seizing from the red;[2]
but in this inn called heaven and earth,
the ten thousand affairs are all like this.
Useless now to reprove the past;
better to make the most of the hours we have.
But don't cut those plum trees in the garden,
don't pull out those garden plants—
they're the ones my father planted.
they're the ones my father watered!
The spring is cold, few vegetables to serve—
I'm ashamed before this guest I've brought.
My guest presents us with a wonderous poem—
who could ever fault such skill?
But I will not praise the words of the poem,
praise instead the truth in it,
for truth has power to delight the living
and move the dead as well.
Ah, father, mother, be my witness,
how could he be a man of "mere firmness"?[3]
Abashed, I read through your poem,
my confidence grown thinner than paper.

2. *Analects* XVII, 18: "The Master said, 'I hate the way purple seizes from red.'" Red, being a primary color, represents the true or upright. Gensei is referring to the social amd political upheavals of the recent past.

3. *Analects* XV, 36: "The Master said, 'The superior man is correctly firm and not firm merely.'" In these closing lines, Gensei follows convention in praising his guest's poem and expressing chagrin that he cannot compose a poem worthy to match it.

Leaving Emyō in Charge: Preface and Poem

(Emyō, originally a monk of the Ritsu sect, joined Gensei's community in 1665 and at this time was Gensei's principal disciple. 5-ch. old style, 1667.)

In the autumn of 1665 I went for the first time to bathe in the hot spring at Arima. It proved effective, and since then I have always wanted to make another visit, constantly gazing far off at the Arima peaks. But my mother is older than ever and I have no brothers who can take care of her for me while I'm gone. So I haven't been able to make the trip. Now, in the spring of 1667, my oldest brother has a vacation and has come from eastern Ōmi for a visit.[1] Accordingly, I told my mother about my desire to make a trip to Arima. She was delighted and gave me her permission. It is the seventh day of the second month of spring and I am ready to set out on the road. Now I address these words to Emyō: The *Book of Odes* says, "Though you have brothers, they're not as good as friends!"[2] And how much better are one's younger associates. I hope you'll take care of things for me. Wishing to make clear my feelings, I have written this poem.

When the Great Way's put in practice,
we'll treat not only our own parents as parents,
but every white head will be our old one,
within the four seas, all our natural kin.
All alike will be filial and brotherly,

1. Motohide, a samurai in the service of the Ii family, lords of the castle of Hikone on the east side of Lake Biwa in Ōmi province.
2. "Lesser Odes," *Ch'ang-ti,* Mao no. 164.

the kind they call Wu-huai's people.[3]
Our doctrine is a miracle of pity and compassion;
with all things we make it be spring.
Vast and wide, the sea of equality—
no "I" in it, no "others" either.
This Way is older than heaven and earth;
Confucian and Buddhist come out of the same dust.
Now I set off on the road to the hot spring,
going to bathe this ailing body.
I leave you behind to look out for my mother—
yours is the purest kind of filial concern.
If you can carry out this charge,
your blessing will equal the Buddha's.

3. Wu-huai was a legendary ruler of high antiquity whose subjects were known for their simple virtue and contentment.

Clouds

(7-ch. *chüeh-chü*, 1667)

Spread like tall canopies, trailing like sashes,
changing shape in the sky's midst, showing no trace of dust,
off to the south, in from the north, nowhere ever lingering,
ten thousand miles of heaven and earth all your neighbors.

Old Man in the Blue

(5-ch. *chüeh-chü*, 1667)

Old Man in the Blue—what a jokester,
winking at us with his clears and cloudies.
But let him flip his hand anyway he wants—
he'll never get at this mind of mine!

Nothing False

(5-ch. *chüeh-chü*, 1667)

> Thoughts all jumbled make a shoddy Dharma;
> ideas that are clear emit wondrous sounds.
> Nothing false in the words I speak—
> you don't believe me, ask your mind!

Poem Without a Category

(5-ch. old style, 1667)

Trailing my stick I go down to the garden edge,
call to a monk to go out the pine gate.
A cup of tea with my mother,
looking at each other, enjoying our tea together.
In the deep lanes, few people in sight;
the dog barks when anyone comes or goes.
Fall floods have washed away the planks of the bridge;
shouldering our sandals, we wade the narrow stream.
By the roadside, a small pavilion
where there used to be a little hill:
it helps out our hermit mood;
country poems pile one sheet on another.
I dabble in the flow, delighted by the shallowness of
    the stream,
gaze at the flagging, admiring how firm the stones are.
The point in life is to know what's enough—
why envy those otherworld immortals?
With the happiness held in one inch-square heart
you can fill the whole space between heaven and earth.

Impromptu at the Fujinomori Shrine

(A Shinto shrine near Gensei's temple. 5-ch. regulated verse, 1667.)

    Autumn light enfolds the trees;
    I've sat so long the dew wets my robe.
    Slanting rays of sun reach in under the pines;
    a light mist drifts beside the bamboo.
    Blossoms of fragrant olive about to burst open,
    maple leaves not yet urging their crimson on us:
    insect voices echo, the twilight breeze is still.
    Deep in poetry musings, I forget to go home.

Oral Composition Aboard a Boat

(7-ch regulated verse, 1667)

Travelers come and go, heading east and west;
if I went by boat ten thousand miles, would the joy ever cease?
Bell sounds near and far beyond the rippling waves;
mountain hues now there, now gone amid the mist and haze.
The sky is chilly over reed shoals, their blossoms prefiguring snow;
waters are cold by willow banks where grasses speak of the wind.
A beautiful scene beyond the reach of words:
one strand of long river swallowing up the sky.

Preface to the Poem on Ten Joys

(The poem itself, since it merely repeats what has been said in the preface, has been omitted.)

Jung Ch'i-ch'i was poor but happy. When Confucius asked him why, he said, "I have three joys. Among the ten thousand things of creation, I have managed to be born a human being. That's my first joy. Men are honored and women looked down on. I have managed to be born a man. That's my second joy. Many people die at an untimely age, but I have lived to be ninety-three. That's my third joy. Poverty is man's constant lot and death is his end. If one lives with the constant and arrives at the end, then what is there to be sad about?"[1]

Ah, Mr. Jung's joys were true joys indeed. But someone like myself has even more joys than he had. How many people are born in this world and live to be a hundred without ever understanding the path by which they come and go, passing through the realm of life and death like drunken men or dreamers, no different from birds or beasts? But I have been fortunate enough to embrace Buddhism and to understand the Way. That is my first joy.

Laymen live in a world of dust and labor, each day farther removed from the Way. But I have left that world to become a monk. That is my second joy.

There are those who, even though they become monks, must work day and night and are no different from laymen. But from the first I have been able to live apart from the world. That is my third joy.

There are those who become followers of the Buddha but, because they are not blessed with a store of good karma

---

1. The opening paragraph is quoted, with some abbreviations, from *Lieh Tzu*, ch. 1.

from the past, content themselves with a lesser version of the doctrine. But I have been fortunate enough to embrace the Mahayana teachings. That is my fourth joy.

Even among followers of the Mahayana, there are those who hear only partial versions of the Buddha's wisdom and do not understand the doctrines that lead to true enlightenment. But I have been fortunate enough to embrace the vehicle that leads to Buddhahood. That is my fifth joy.

Even among those who embrace the vehicle that leads to Buddhahood, there are those who hear the doctrine that the mind itself can produce Buddhahood but still fail to realize the even more marvelous fact that they themselves are Buddhas. I fortunately have understood it. That is my sixth joy.

I have been born a human being and a man, and I have already passed the age of forty, so I have escaped the fate of dying young. I do not envy Mr. Jung his great age.

That makes nine joys. And on top of all that, I have one truly great joy. Many people lose their father and mother while they are still children and spend their whole lives as orphans with no one to turn to. My father lived to the age of eighty-six and died peacefully. This year my mother too has turned eighty-six. And although she is ill and I fear the end may come any time now, still it is an occasion for joy and surely not for sadness.

How much more so when I think that, in the twenty years since I retired from secular life, when I lived sometimes in the bustling city, sometimes in the hills and woods, I have been like a shadow following a form, never once separated from my parents' side. Surely this is a greater joy than any that Mr. Jung could boast.

With these ten joys, how could I fail to be happy? Now I have only this wish. I have grown old living far off among these clouds and hills and in the course of this life I have at last attained enlightenment. In my next life, I must use this understanding of the Dharma realm to save as many living beings as I can. That is the only thing that I desire now.

A Gift of Orchids: Preface and Poem

(5-ch. old style, 1667)

I once planted a large field with orchids, but because of wind and frost they all withered and died. I hated to lose them and thought if I stuck the roots in the ground, they might eventually come up and blossom again. But I didn't really take care of them or watch how they were doing.

In Fushimi there is an elderly doctor whose name is Yoshizawa. He is very advanced in years and has a thorough knowledge of his profession. Whenever anyone in our religious group, young or old, is taken sick, we always call on him, and hence he has occasion to come here from time to time. One day he happened to glance out at the garden, saw the orchids, and said, "What are those nice plants doing out there as though someone had thrown them away? I'd like to get some of them and try raising them—would that be possible?"

I was delighted and said, "Please help yourself!" I asked him to take them away as soon as it was convenient, and then several months went by. This fall he was taken ill and died. Now whenever I look at the orchids I think of him and feel sorrowful. So I decided I would like to present them to his family.

Long ago in China the nobleman Chi-tzu of Yen-ling happened to visit the lord of Hsü. He knew that the lord of Hsü wanted the sword he was wearing, and in his mind he agreed to give it to him at a later date. But before he could do so, the lord of Hsü died. So he hung the sword on a tree on the gravemound, saying, "How could I go against what I had promised him in my heart just because he had died!"

I feel even more strongly about the matter than Chi-tzu

did, since I actually told Dr. Yoshizawa in so many words that he could have the orchids.

Dr. Yoshizawa has two sons. The elder, named Yoshinobu, is already carrying on his father's business and is practicing medicine very diligently. Recently he visited our temple, and in the course of the conversation I told him about the orchids. "They are in a way a memento of your father, something that he loved," I said. "Why don't you try planting and raising them?"

"You're right," said the son, looking very solemn. "I'll move them tomorrow."

In the end I composed a short poem in old style to present to him along with the orchids. Those who have departed we can never see again, but at least we can see the things that they loved and left behind.

> Trailing leaves—cut them but you'll seldom kill them;
> vital roots—plant them, though they're easily injured.
> I have tended orchids, nine acres full,[1]
> loving the fragrance they give to my room.
> If I should fall ill, they make good medicine;
> when hot days come, they spread a clear cool.
> Who says that when autumn winds appear
> they'll wipe out this teeming fragrance?
> I will trust to a few surviving rootstalks,
> watch over them, desiring to see them flourish.[2]

1. The line closely parallels one in the poem *Li sao* or "Encountering Sorrow" by the Chinese poet Ch'ü Yüan (c. 300 B.C.).

2. The "few surviving rootstalks" are Dr. Yoshizawa's two sons.

Poem in Rhyme-Prose Form on the Caged Bird, with Preface

In the fall of the year with the cyclical sign *kanoto-ushi* (1661), I accompanied my mother on a trip to Owari. In the inn where we stayed there was a sparrow in a cage. I asked if I could turn it loose, but the host of the inn said, "I'm just keeping it for somebody else. It doesn't belong to me." Much distressed, I had to give up the idea. Finally I wrote this poem in *fu* or rhyme-prose form on the caged bird in order to comfort myself. I have used the five words "caged" "bird" "longs" for its "old" "forest" as my rhymes. I have borrowed the device of having someone appear in a dream and expound his views, a device handed down to us from the poets of past times.

Let me ask you, sparrow,
what day you left your branches?
With those leafy hills of yours,
how did you come to be caged?
In the meanness of your narrow cage,
you've not forgotten your soaring flights,
but chirping, chirping, you hop about alone,
helpless as a fish in a cooking pot.
Pitying you, I said to the host,
"This wild bird here,
his call's so common,
his form so small,
he's hardly worth admiring—
why not return him to his treetop?"
The host replied,
"It's not that I have no feelings

but I'm keeping him for someone else—
I wouldn't dare turn him loose."
I said nothing more
but remained alone with my cheerless thoughts.
That night I dreamed of a person
who yet did not have a person's face.
He bowed to me and said,
"Old karma drags me down,
till I end up in a cage.
If it weren't for you, who would help me?
Still, I have my thoughts—
listen while I warble a while:
Our sojourn in these three worlds [1]
is brief as dew or lightning.
That faroff forest of old—
how is it worth longing for?
When I look at human beings
I see them forever tangled in love,
their hearts without a moment of peace.
They can't see that it's all illusion,
that here in this burning house
they are like persons scorched or seared.
Headlong they race after profit and fame,
and in the end are reborn to the same fate.
And I in my dwelling here,
what have I to envy, what to regret?
My cramped and narrow cage
is in fact as wide as the universe.
I needn't worry about hunger or thirst
or fear the eagle or the hawk.
The body I have now
is the same one I had of old.
Pain and joy go with us everywhere—

---

1. The worlds of desire, form, and formlessness, the realms of beings who have not yet gained enlightenment.

we have only to live out our years.
The vastness of heaven and earth
is no vaster than this mind of mine.
Here within my cage
are groves of gardenias,
here inside my cage
are sandalwood breezes.
Why would I long to be the great P'eng bird,
flailing the wind, plotting his southward journey?[2]
I ignored the precepts in a past existence,
so I've been born a flying creature,
but because I pursued wisdom diligently
I've come on a person who understands me.
Better that I endure these sparrow hops
and end my life in this cage.
Now and hereafter
I hope you'll inquire of me no more!"
Suddenly I woke from my dream;
birds were singing, insects chirring,
but propped on my pillow, all I could hear
was the drip drip of the waterclock.

2. The huge bird described in the first section of *Chuang Tzu*.

PROSE
SELECTIONS

Preface to *The Inquiring about Illness Collection*

Around the second month of summer this year, the dampness and mountain mist once more troubled me so much that I was tossing and turning in bed. It was not the kind of thing that I could rid myself of through the power of meditation, and so I sent for a doctor. My six or seven boys brought me my medicine, and when they did so, asked me, "What should we do to comfort an ailing bodhisattva?"

I said, "Why don't each of you try writing a poem to describe your thoughts. It will give me pleasure to see what's on your mind."

Accordingly they drew lots for the rhymes they would use and responded to each other's poems. We met seven days in the residence hall here and one day at the Gokuraku-ji, so that with the two places, it made eight meetings, and the collection of poems made up a small volume.

The boys then requested me to give the collection a title. I said, "Long ago the Bodhisattva Manjushri went to call on the layman Vimalakirti to inquire about his illness, and he recorded the questions and answers in the section of the Vimalakirti Sutra entitled 'Inquiring about Illness.'[1] Now this collection is rather similar in nature, so why don't we call it 'The Inquiring about Illness Collection.'"

The boys replied, "This is the sort of thing that makes us wonder if our teacher isn't somewhat dense! It would be

---

1. Vimalakirti, a wealthy merchant and lay believer in Buddhism in India in the time of the Buddha, is the subject of the Vimalakirti Sutra. He was remarkable for his piety and religious understanding; his name Vimalakirti means "Renowned as Undefiled." The Buddha, hearing that he was sick, sent the Bodhisattva Manjushri to inquire how he was, and they engaged in the famous dialogue recorded in section 5 of the sutra, "Manjushri Inquires about Illness."

all right, perhaps, for you to compare yourself to Vimalakirti. But how could we possibly presume to put ourselves in a category with Manjushri!"

I said, "I'm already provided with an 'undefiled' mind such as Vimalakirti had, and you are equipped with the nature of a Manjushri. He was a son of the Buddha and you are sons of the Buddha. Why should you be in such awe of Manjushri?

"These poems and hymns of yours can't of course bear comparison with the refined thought and profound talent of those two sages. And yet they all come forth from the sea of a nature that is undefiled and in perfect harmony with all things. Looking at the waves on that sea, we find that some are shallow and others deep, some widely spaced, some closely spaced—but that's the only difference.

"What is undefiled and in perfect harmony with all things is virtuous. What is deep and dense is meritorious. Where there is virtue, there must be merit. If you apply yourselves to meditation, training, effort and practice, and do so day after day, month after month, then eventually you'll reach the stage of depth and density. Why worry that at present you are 'shallow and widely spaced'?

"How much more is this true of those who delight in the teachings of perfect harmony. Though they have eyes of flesh, these will be Buddha eyes; though they have a commonplace mind, it will be a Buddha mind. The realm that the Buddha eyes behold, the writings that are born from the Buddha mind—even the merest report of such things is far superior to the doctrines of the Buddha Vairochana concerning the various categories of being.[2]

"Haven't you heard it said that the wonderful Good

---

2. "Teachings of perfect harmony" here refers to the Lotus Sutra, which promises immediate salvation for all beings. The Buddha Vairochana, on the other hand, is associated with other sutras and schools of thought that describe various stages of enlightenment or define certain categories of persons that can never achieve enlightenment.

Hard Tree, even while it is still below ground, puts up shoots over an area of a hundred spans, and the sweet-toned kalavinka, even while it is a chick in the shell, already surpasses in voice all the other kinds of birds. If you still don't believe me, then go climb up Mount Wu-t'ai and ask Manjushri himself!"[3]

3. Mount Wu-t'ai in northern China was the center of a cult devoted to Manjushri, who was believed to dwell there eternally.

Record of a Climb Up Inari Hill

Inari Hill is a peak near me. When I go out my door, its heap of emerald seems close enough to pick up in my hands. I had long heard that it was a spot of unusual beauty, and of course I knew that from ancient times recluses and eccentric monks have lived in the caves there. I am by nature a great lover of mountains and rivers and historical places. Why in the world, then, have I lived here on Grass Hill for seven or eight years without ever climbing it?

One day Kada Nobuaki and Ōnishi Chikamitsu[1] of Inari Hill came to invite me to make the climb. Mr. Kada's two sons led the way and the rest of us followed along behind. We threaded among the pines, walking on a stone pathway that skirted the edge of a pond. The reflections of the pines looked like dragons or serpents and the clear jade-green water made us feel refreshed. By the time we had climbed halfway up the hill we were tired, so we gathered in the shade of the trees and rested. I was particularly weary, and I stretched out with a rock for my couch and stayed there a long time before getting up again. The distant mountains resembled a painting and it was an ideal spot for lying down and relaxing.

From there we set out again, pulling our way up peaks, peering down into hollows, passing between walls of rock, until we descended into a ravine. On the walls of the ravine there were signs where shrines to various gods had stood. The place is called Deity Ravine. In it are maple trees of the kind known as Inari Hill maples. In old times there was a waterfall here, but the mountain has become overgrown, the stream has dried up, and there's no waterfall there now.

---

1. On Kada Nobuaki, see p. 20. I have been unable to find any information on Ōnishi Chikamitsu.

Nevertheless, water from some hidden source keeps drip-dripping down endlessly like a kimono sash. In time of drought, the village people rap on the rock and beg for rain, and they invariably get a response. This would not be so if there were not some spiritual being there. How could the water ever dry up? Alongside the water is a place called Cell Cliff because long ago there was a monk's cell there.

Leaving the ravine, we clambered up a height that was as steep and sheer as a palm turned sideways. After each step we would stop to get our breath, and our lips became parched. There was no water around, but it was the season for rock pears,[2] and many of them were ripe, so we ate these and found they relieved our thirst. Certain members of the group, however, began to regret having come along on such a strenuous trip.

We continued climbing up and down, the flights of stone steps rough and craggy. When we reached the top of the steps we came on a rock that had the most strange and astonishing shape. When I asked about it, I was told it is called Thunder Rock. Long ago a hermit monk put a curse on the thunder and imprisoned it in the rock, hence the name. I thought to myself, this hermit monk must be Jōzō.[3] His biography says that he lived for a time on Inari Hill, where he ordered the spirit boy of the hill to bring him flowers and water for use as offerings. That's how I know it must have been he.

Having reached the top of the hill, we could see the mountains and rivers to the east, west, and south, and the city to the north, just as though we were perched on a couch and peering down at a little garden pool. It was in fact one of the finest spots in the world.

---

2. *Iwanashi* or *Epigaea asiatica,* a low-growing edible berry.

3. A monk of the Tendai sect who lived 892 to 964. He received religious training at Mt. Hiei and later lived at other mountains in the area. Many stories are told of his miraculous powers.

The hill has three peaks, lined up in diminishing height, the sites of what used to be the Upper, Middle, and Lower shrines respectively.[4] I had heard that there was once an "incarnation" cedar here[5] and that, though the cedar was now gone, one could still see the place where it had stood. But at the time the story slipped my mind and I forgot to ask about it.

After coming back down the hill, we stopped at the pond and composed poems before going home. When I got home, I presented my mother with some rock pears and azaleas I had gathered.

---

4. As Gensei indicates, the Inari shrines, founded early in the eighth century, were originally on top of the three peaks. Later the main shrine was moved to the foot of the hill, though the whole hill remains dotted with shrines. Inari was initially a rice deity but in later centuries came to be looked on as the patron deity of business activities. The Fushimi Inari Shrine is the headquarters for all the Inari shrines throughout Japan.

5. A tree believed to be an incarnation of a god or Buddha. At present there are a number of large *sugi* or Japanese cedars on the hill that are the object of worship.

Record of a Return Visit to Takagamine

(The piece is in five sections; the following is the second section, describing a Buddhist retreat called the Jōkō-an or Hut of Pure Light in the region of Takagamine, a hill northwest of Kyoto. See p. 8. Written in 1663, when Gensei was recuperating from illness.)

The Hut of Pure Light has nothing but hills close to it and in the distance. Distant and wonderful are the numerous heights of Kitayama; distant and imposing are the ranged peaks of Mount Hiei. Close by and holy in nature is the hill of the Thunder God's shrine; close by and of great beauty is the White Cloud Ravine. If you climb up the ravine, you come to a Buddhist hall that would fit right into a picture. In fact, the whole scene looks just like a screen painting.

Anyone who lives here is beyond the green hills, and there are no houses or rice fields to confront his eye. Although he is not actually very far away, it's just as though he were in a remote valley deep in the mountains. I'm much attracted to the spot.

Generally speaking, if you choose to live too high up, then the cities and houses, suburbs and country villages will be no more than a vague blur beyond your eyelashes. You can get a general view of them, but it's up to you whether you want to have anything to do with them or not. If the place where you live is too low down, on the other hand, then the shouts and angry voices, the drums and songs can be an annoyance or a downright evil. If you're a person with weak powers of concentration, how can you help but find your mind being distracted by them?

This place, however, is not too high up and not too low down. Here you couldn't keep yourself entirely aloof from the world even if you wanted to, but neither could you be distracted by it. Such a dwelling accords with the principle of the Middle Way.[1] I believe that when people are pursuing the religious life, if they are too high up, they cut themselves off from the secular world, while if they are too low down, they become entangled in it. But if they can steer a middle course, seeking to learn from those above them and instructing those below them, then they will be close to the ideal. I want to make a special note of this point so I will have it to refer to when my illness improves.

1. An important principle in Buddhism, which rejects both hedonism and extreme asceticism.

The Biography of the Mountain Man of Mist Valley

(The piece imitates the form of biographies in the Chinese official histories and, like them, ends with a section called "Appraisal." The reader should have little difficulty guessing the identity of the Mountain Man.)

I don't know where the mountain man came from. When I asked him his name, he said, "My family name is Mountain and my given name Man." He used to have his home on Grass Hill and took great delight in strolling around Mist Valley—that's where his name came from.

He loved to read books. It didn't matter what the book was, if he happened on a book he hadn't read, he immediately bought it. He came from a poor family, so he was always owing money for books.

He suffered by nature from a number of illnesses and dreaded the cold. In the course of a year, he was really only comfortable during the summer months. But when he was reading a book, he would be perfectly happy and forget about his ailments.

He always used to say, "The world of phenomena[1] is my mind, and mind is my world of phenomena. The world of phenomena and mind have never been two different things. The precepts are my house, meditation is my robe, and wisdom my food. With these I take my ease in the world of phenomena."[2]

---

1. *Hokkai;* the term has a number of meanings, but Gensei probably intends it to mean the world of phenomena as perceived by the mind. The point here is that there should be no separation between the perceiver and the things perceived.

2. The precepts (*kai*), meditation (*jō*), and wisdom (*e*) constitute the *sangaku* or three types of learning that cover all the aspects of Buddhist doctrine and practice.

Appraisal: There are two kinds of illness, illness of the mind and illness of the body. If you're ill in mind, the most marvelous physician can't do anything for you.[3] The mountain man was ill in body only. With the mind of the world of phenomena, how could he have been really ill? Lucky for him!

---

3. Gensei is of course not referring to mental illness but rather to spiritual ignorance or blindness.

Account of the Life of Giō of Grass Hill

In ancient times it was customary to praise men of outstanding virtue by saying that even the ruler would not venture to treat them as subjects, and even their fathers would not venture to treat them as sons.

Giō was a true man of the Way. Everyone in our religious group spoke highly of him. In addition, he was only one year younger than me. Consequently, I always regarded him with respect and affection and thought of him as a friend. I never ventured to treat him as a disciple. And now I am writing this account of the facts of his life because it is my duty as a friend to do so—indeed, I could hardly do less.

Giō's personal name as a monk was Nikka and he used the literary name Chikuan. His surname was Okada and he was a native of Marugame in the province of Sanuki.[1] His father's personal name was Yoshikatsu. His mother was of the Inoue family.

When Giō was young, his father for no particular reason drove his mother out of the house. She went away with some people, drifting from place to place until in time she fell sick in the province of Settsu and was confined to her bed. Giō went and nursed her there. Eventually, when he realized that she would never be well again, he helped her to return to Takamatsu, her native city, where she died. He buried her there, grieving deeply, and returned to his father. At that time he was seventeen.

---

1. A castle town on the northern coast of Shikoku in present-day Kagawa prefecture. In a lament for Giō's father (SZS ch. 12, p. 180), Gensei says that Giō came from "a wealthy family of Sanuki" but gives no details.

His father in time remarried, and Giō showed the same kind of filial respect toward his stepmother. Later, his father drove his stepmother out of the house as well. Giō became more unhappy than ever.

Giō was by nature fond of learning, a fact that did not please his father. Hence he would always read in secret, fearful that his father would discover what he was doing. Eventually his father found out and, as Giō had feared, expelled him from the house. Having no other course, he came to Kyoto. At this time he began to think seriously of leaving secular life and becoming a monk.

In the first year of the Jōō era (1652), when he was twenty-eight, Giō shaved his head and placed himself under the guidance of Gizui of the western hills. Later, when Gizui went on a trip to eastern Japan, Giō placed himself under Setsudō of the Kōshō-ji.[2] There he listened to expositions of the *Engaku* Sutra and came to understand the subtle meaning of the Heart Sutra.

In the winter of the following year, through the introduction of a certain secretary in the imperial court of justice, he came to me and placed himself under my direction. At that time I was living in temporary quarters in a temple in Kyoto. After three or four months, he said to me, "I would like to have you for my permanent teacher. I want to change to the vestments of your sect." At this time he abandoned the Zen teachings and became a believer in our kind of Buddhism. He spent the following days reading the Lotus Sutra and each day embraced some new doctrine he had learned from the text.

While still in secular life, he had been very fond of the teachings of Wang Yang-ming, and these habits of thought

---

2. A temple of the Jōdo Shin sect located at Horikawa Shichijō in Kyoto. From what is said later, however, it appears that Giō was at this time not a follower of Shin Buddhism but of Zen teachings.

remained with him still.³ Hence he was inclined to turn immediately to the writings of Wang Yang-ming, such as the *Collected Writings* or *Instructions for Practical Living*, and then demand of me to know how the Buddhist doctrine of the identity of phenomena and noumena fitted in with them. I laughed and said, "Confucianism is only one small part of our doctrine. It's not worth arguing with you at this stage. After you've spent a long time at your studies and have a thorough understanding of our doctrines, you'll understand it by yourself."

A few years later, Giō happened to be accompanying me on a visit to Takatsuki in Settsu when he suddenly announced one evening, "I have for the first time realized how Confucianism and Buddhism agree and how they differ. From now on I will concentrate on the study of the sacred texts of India." After that, his books on "good knowledge" were consigned to the shelf and were soon buried in dust.

In the first year of the Meireki era (1655) Giō, who was then thirty-one, moved with me to Mist Valley. Though it is a considerable distance from Kyoto, he went to the city to beg for alms and never complained of getting tired. Walking or standing still, sitting or sleeping, he manifested a cheerful delight in the practice of the Way.

Earlier, when Giō was staying in a certain temple in Kyoto, his wife, whom he had left behind in Sanuki, unable to overcome her love and longing for him, came to Kyoto with her mother. Hovering outside the gate, she got one of the people in the temple to take in a message saying that someone had come from Sanuki looking for Giō and requesting an interview with him. Giō, unaware of who the visitor might be, came to the gate in person. When he

---

3. Wang Yang-ming (1472–1529), a Chinese Neo-Confucian philosopher of the Ming dynasty, stressed man's innate moral sense, which he referred to as "good knowledge," and the need to put one's beliefs into practice.

looked, he saw it was his wife. He showed no trace of reproach, but in a polite manner said, "I'm sorry you've come such a long way on my account. I ought to invite you in to rest and refresh yourself, but I'm afraid women are not allowed inside the gate here. I hope you'll excuse me if I leave you now." So saying, he went back into the temple. His wife, shamefaced but at the same time resentful, went back to Sanuki.

Though Giō had thus cut off his ties with the world, he was never able to forget about his father and constantly grieved that he had gone against his father's commands. From time to time he would kneel and, all alone, would recite with great fervor the *Classic of Filial Piety*.

Once his father happened to come to Kyoto in connection with some affair. Giō, trusting to luck, went one day to the house where his father was staying and asked for the master of the house, who was an old friend of the family. Several times he persuaded the master of the house to convey a message to his father, but his father refused to respond. Day after day Giō paced back and forth in front of the gate, unable to tear himself away. He would go in the morning and not come back until evening, continuing this for a period of some ten days. When his father finally went back to Sanuki, Giō secretly followed him as far as Osaka, where he wept tears of farewell.

It was continually on his mind that his father was advanced in years and had no one to look out for him, and he therefore wrote to his relatives at home urging them to do what they could. He also pleaded with his stepmother, who at this time was living in Kyoto with her daughter, and finally persuaded the two of them to return to live with his father.

Some time later, his father was suddenly taken ill and died. When word reached Giō, he spent the next three days without eating. Only after all those around him had remonstrated with him did he at last consent to take a little gruel.

His relatives arrived from Sanuki and pressed him to return, but he told them, "I have already left my family and become a monk—how could I possibly go home again? Moreover, while my father was alive he accused me of a fault and never forgave me. Now that he is no longer here, would I try to cheat him by becoming his heir? Fortunately my younger sister is living at home with my mother. I hope you good people will help to find her a suitable husband so that he can carry on my father's line. That is my real wish."

In the end, he refused to go with them. Later he received word that his younger half sister had married and that her husband had taken over the management of the household. In the spring of the following year (1658), he made a trip home to pay respects at his father's grave.

In the first year of the Kambun era (1661), in the fourth month, Giō was taken slightly ill while in Takatsuki. In the middle of the fifth month he went to Kyoto to receive medical attention. He returned from Kyoto on the first day of the sixth month and took up temporary lodging in Gyokusen-in, a temple on a nearby hill.

On the morning of the fifth day, he called all his friends together to say goodby to them. Straightening his clerical robes and spreading out his mat, he faced the Buddha and performed three ritual prostrations. Then he joined with the others in reciting the *Juryō* chapter of the Lotus Sutra.[4] After three more ritual prostrations, he returned to his seat.

When he felt that the end was near, he said to his friends, "Since I became a monk, I have carried out the practices leading to nirvana without any omissions and for ten years have found joy in the Way. And I have always thought that throughout all heaven and earth, there's no place I would exchange for this one. Its winds and mists, its

---

4. The *Juryō* chapter, ch. 16, in which the Buddha reveals that he attained enlightenment countless aeons in the past, is one of the chapters singled out for special veneration in the Nichiren sect.

hills and streams are my dwelling. What reason would I have to leave this place and go off looking for some Land of Tranquil Light elsewhere?"

The other monks at his side asked him to compose a final verse to leave behind, but Giō laughed and said, "The few words I have just spoken will do as my farewell address to the world."

Sometime later, his whole body was suddenly wracked with pain and he cried out in a voice so loud that it startled everyone around. After a long time, he recovered consciousness and, when asked what had happened, replied, "Without realizing what I was doing, I dropped off into a pleasant sleep, that was all." The rest of the night he chatted quietly, and then all at once died. Actually, the end came at sunup on the sixth day.

While he was laid out in preparation for the funeral, his appearance was just the same as when he had been alive and there was a gentle smile on his face. His age was thirty-seven and he had been a monk for ten summers. Everyone expressed regret that he could not have lived to a greater age.

Giō was diligent and untiring in his pursuit of learning, and his love for and devotion to the Way left nothing to be desired.

Once he was accompanying me when we were crossing the Gojō Bridge over the Kamo River in Kyoto. At that time the north wind was blowing fiercely, but Giō contrived to walk beside me in such a way that he sheltered me with his body. All his daily actions were like this. He was a simple and forthright person who made no particular effort to ingratiate himself with others. Those meeting him for the first time found him difficult to approach, though as they got to know him better they were impressed by his sincerity. As a result, there were very few people who really understood him.

All his life he lived in honest poverty. Among his belongings he did not even have the three robes permitted to all monks, much less anything else. From time to time he wrote poems in Chinese or composed Japanese *waka* but, searching for them now, I can't seem to find copies of very many of them. He also kept a record of things that he had seen or heard, which he titled *Chikuan's Random Notes*.[5]

---

5. Gensei made a collection of Giō's writings entitled *Chikuan ikō* or "Chikuan's Posthumous Works," to which he wrote a preface; it was published in 1663. The large number of works by Gensei and his associates that were published and the rapidity with which they got into print is an indication of the growing importance of commercial printing in the Kyoto area at this time. See Keene, *World Within Walls*, p. 4.

Composing Poems

When I'm sick I like to compose poems to amuse myself. Someone said to me, "I'm afraid you'll overtax your energy. I wish you'd take up some other pastime!"

I replied, "My illness comes from depression of the spirits and composing poems helps to dispel it. It's like a chess player who has no skill at the game but just lets his hand move anywhere it wants to. He has no real objective in playing the game—he simply wants to enjoy himself. When I compose poems, it's the same way. I certainly don't overtax my energy!

"Moreover, a monk should concern himself with the precepts, meditation and wisdom, and composing poems is one manifestation of wisdom. As a rule, anyone who is a monk ought to confine his diversions to matters that relate to these three concerns. Why should I take up some other pursuit?"

Feeding the Dog

At the foot of the hill there's a dog named Little White. He's a puppy of the dog that belongs to the keeper of the Shōshin-an, where my mother lives. Every once in a while he comes around, acting very friendly. One day he came just at mealtime and stood by the eaves whining. His voice sounded very pitiful. When my mother heard it, she said, "That's Little White's voice. What a pathetic whine! He lives with a poor family and I guess he's hungry. I wonder if anybody will give him anything to eat?"

She kept on worrying about it, and when evening came, she gave him some food from her own tray. At the same time she said to the people who wait on her, "I'm sure you think charity just means giving alms to people. But animals don't have any understanding of language, so even when they're hungry, they can't tell anyone about it. They're much more to be pitied than people. From now on, please see that he's taken care of."

I happened to be in my mother's room at the time, and when I observed this, I recalled the following incident. The Buddha's disciple Shariputra once presented a bowl of rice to the Buddha. After the Buddha had finished accepting it, he gave it to a dog. Then he asked Shariputra, "Which act do you think merits greater blessing, your giving me an offering of rice, or my giving it to the dog?" Shariputra replied, "As I see it, the Buddha's giving the offering to the dog is an act that merits greater blessing. It is only natural to pay honor to the Buddha, the highest of beings. It can't compare to the Buddha's giving alms to a dog, because the latter is an expression of a compassionate heart."

This incident is recorded in the *Daichido-ron*.[1] My

---

1. The *Mahaprajnaparamitopodesha* attributed to Nagarjuna, a 100-chapter encyclopedic work. The incident Gensei refers to appears in *Daichido-ron* ch. 32, *Taishō Daizōkyō* vol. 25, p. 301.

mother's view on the matter happened to correspond exactly to this passage. I was so impressed that in the end I made a record of the event.

The year with the cyclical sign *mizunoto-u* (1663), first month of spring, the day of the Dog. It is just a coincidence that this happens to be the day of the Dog?

Preface to the "Matching Poems of a Holy Man and a Plain Man"

Huang T'ing-chien praised T'ao Yüan-ming by saying, "Yüan-ming did not make poems—he depicted the wonders that were in his heart, that was all."[1] The wonders that are in the heart—these are the true inner nature (*seirei*) of poetry. If one is not able to lose himself in poetry, then how can he attain such heights? It is like forgetting about your voice and being good at singing, forgetting your body and being good at dancing. Only when you have reached the stage where you have forgotten about poetry can you begin to talk about poems.[2] Huang T'ing-chien understood the wonders of T'ao Yüan-ming's art, but he was not able to employ Yüan-ming's art in his own poetry. Instead he used up ten thousand rolls of paper trying to outdo this word or that phrase of Li Po or Tu Fu.[3] It is a difficult thing to forget about poetry!

Whenever I read the poems of Han-shan and Shih-te, I admire the wondrous quality of their poetry. This may be

---

1. Huang T'ing-chien (1045–1105), an outstanding poet of the Sung dynasty, was especially admired in Japan by the Zen monks of the Kamakura and Muromachi period. T'ao Yüan-ming or T'ao Ch'ien (365-427) is noted for his simple but deeply philosophical depictions of rural life. The statement is found in the *Hou-shan shih-hua*, a collection of remarks on poetry compiled by Ch'en Shih-tao (1053–1102), but it is attributed there to Su Tung-p'o (1037–1101).

2. Gensei has in mind the famous passage in *Chuang Tzu*, ch. 26: "Words exist because of meaning; once you've gotten the meaning, you can forget the words. Where can I find a man who has forgotten words so I can have a word with him."

3. Huang T'ing-chien's poetry is markedly derivative in nature; he was particularly assiduous in imitating the style and diction of Tu Fu.

called the Supreme Vehicle of poetry.[4] This is what it means to "forget poetry." It is not the kind of thing that later imitators have been able to come even close to. These two men may be called the T'ao Yüan-mings of Buddhist poetry.

In the past I have several times thought that I would try making imitations of a few of their poems, but I never got around to doing anything about it. This year, around the end of the second month of autumn, my mother was taken ill, and it was ten days or more before she recovered. I regularly looked in on her at mealtimes and waited on her for a number of days. But my mother by nature prefers to be alone. She customarily stays in her room, spending all day facing the Buddha, and does not like to have others around. I would therefore withdraw from the room and go sit on the west verandah, looking at the mountains in silence. And from time to time I happened to recall the poems of these two masters.

Unlike the poems of Han-shan, those of Shih-te number no more than forty or fifty. So I decided to try writing poems using the same rhyme words. Some days I wrote ten or twenty poems, some days only six or seven. I said what came out of my mouth and wrote down what my hand felt like writing. In some cases I matched both the rhymes and the ideas of the original poems, in other cases I matched only the rhymes but not the ideas, depending on how I felt. Since Shih-te's poems total only 58, after a few days I had finished.

One of the young boys said to me, "In the past there have been writers who imitated the poems of Han-shan.[5] Why now, Master, do you just match phrases with the poems of Shih-te?"

I replied, "I have heard that Han-shan was a reincarnation of Manjushri and Shih-te a reincarnation of Saman-

---

4. Gensei uses the word "vehicle" in the Buddhist sense to mean a doctrine or teaching.

5. E.g., the noted Sung poet Wang An-shih (1021–1086).

tabhadra.⁶ I have from birth been hampered by my scanty wisdom and so have not been able to attain enlightenment. I am as frightened by wisdom as I am fearful of a raging fire. If it were a matter of wisdom, I would hesitate to apply even to Manjushri for help. The only thing I aspire to attain now is just the religious practice and devotion of Samantabhadra. I would like to establish some connection with this bodhisattva, slight though it may be. It is not just because the poems of Shih-te are few in number that I have chosen to write sequels to them."

The boy said, "Well then, who will you share these poems with? *We* certainly couldn't understand them, could we?"

"Why not?" I replied. "You have not yet fully experienced or understood what it means to see the Buddha nature within you. But you are not on the level of ordinary unenlightened beings. And the same applies in the case of poetry. Though you have not yet reached that wondrous stage where you know the real inner nature of poetry, still you are already to be numbered among the followers of poetry's holy way. If you just have faith in that, you can talk about poetry as well as anyone else!"⁷

The year *hinoe-uma* (1666), autumn, the ninth day of the ninth month; written by the Son of the Mystic Law of Mist Valley on the west verandah of the Yōju-an.⁸

---

6. The statement is attributed to Feng-kan and is found in the preface by Lü-ch'iu Yin to the collected poems of Han-shan, Shih-te, and Feng-kan, the *San-yin shih-chi*. See my *Cold Mountain: 100 Poems by the T'ang Poet Han-shan* (New York: Columbia University Press, 1962), p. 7. The bodhisattva Manjushri is the symbol of wisdom, the bodhisattva Samantabhadra the symbol of religious practice.

7. The custom of likening degrees of poetic understanding and ability to levels of religious enlightenment in Buddhism derives from the *Ts'ang-lang shih-hua* or "Ts'ang-lang's Remarks on Poetry" by the Chinese critic Yen Yü (fl. 1180–1235).

8. The separate residence that Gensei built for his mother in 1661 just west of his own quarters. It became a nunnery after her death in 1667. Myōshi or Son of the Mystic [Law] is one of Gensei's literary names.

Inscription at the End of the Poem Scrolls

The Inari Shrine is hardly a bull's bellow[1] away from my temple in Mist Valley. The head priest, Kada Nobuaki, is a young man who likes refined pastimes, and not just those native to Japan. For some years we have visited back and forth and have struck up a rare kind of friendship. It's largely because we live so close to each other and because, as the saying goes, we "smell alike."

This year in the second month of winter, we happened to get together with four or five friends to compose *waka*. After we had written *waka*, we went on to write *kanshi*. Each person then took his compositions and mounted them on a scroll. By the time the last month of winter came around, we had met a total of three times.

I sighed and said, "Ah, in our present age of shallow customs and vapid personalities, people no longer care about refined pastimes. Even among those who have some slight interest in such things, the people who speak out on the subject of poetry in Chinese never say a word about *waka*, and those who talk about *waka* never speak about *kanshi*. The two groups deride and laugh at each other, looking upon one another as belonging to enemy factions. They fail to realize that the way of poetry is grounded in the human heart. Chinese and Japanese poetry may use different words, but they are alike in the various sentiments they express.

"To be sure, when a bunch of shrike-tongued persons like ourselves attempt to behave like mountain birds warbling in spring or meadow insects chirping in autumn, one

---

1. *Krosha*, an Indian land measure, the area within which a bull's cry may be heard; roughly, a mile or two. On the Inari Shrine and Kada Nobuaki, see p. 20.

may question whether the results even deserve to be called *kanshi* or *waka*. More to the point, one may ask why such poems should be set down in ink on paper, to purchase for their authors nothing more than a handful of laughs.

"Nevertheless, in an age bereft of gold and jewels, even copper and iron may come to be looked on as precious. In this muddy world we live in, it is a pleasure just to compose poems all by oneself, so how much more so when there are several of us doing it together? It is a delight to produce merely one poem, so how much more so to produce a number of them? And if we seem to be as fond of them as of the old worn-out family broom, should that surprise you?"

I have added this brief note to Mr. Kada's scroll.

Grave Inscription for the Two Boys Zenkyū and Jōkan: with Preface

The two boys were sons of the family named Nakano living in Fushimi in Yamashiro province. In the spring of this year (1667), when the elder boy was eight and the younger boy four, they both came down with smallpox. On the twentieth day of the first month of spring the elder boy died, and the younger one died on the twenty-seventh day. The father wailed and cried, cursing Heaven and longing for his sons.

The father once said to me, "I am from a merchant family and I can never break away from wordly tasks and entanglements. But I am determined that when my boys grow up, the elder will study medicine and the younger will become a monk. They're not going to carry on my business!" The younger boy had in fact already been promised to a certain temple.

The older boy was unconscious when he died, but the younger one remained clear in his mind right up to the end. He put his palms together and recited the *daimoku*[1] twenty or thirty times. Then his voice broke off and his breathing stopped.

The father felt even worse over the death of the younger boy. Then after a while he seemed to reach his own understanding of what had happened. "Ah—it is my fault. Heaven has in fact done this because of me," he said. "Ever since I brought the two boys into the world I have day after day been seeking and have never been satisfied. Now that the

---

1. *Nam-myōhō-renge-kyō,* the chant employed by followers of Nichiren Buddhism.

boys are gone, my heart and mind can be at rest. Now even if I had millions in cash, who would I have to enjoy it with? The best thing is to lessen my desires. With fewer desires, I won't notice that I am poor. If my boys had lived, even if they had treated me with the utmost filial devotion, they could not have brought me this joy. My two boys are true models of filial piety, for they have in this way freed me from care."

One day a certain person came and asked me if I would write a grave inscription for the two boys. I was moved by the story, which I have recounted here, and composed the following inscription:

> A father sired two sons,
> and having won this blessing, he wanted more.
> Had the older son been a skilled physician
> he could not have cured this fault;
> had the younger become a monk
> he could not have cleansed such desire.
> But when one morning the two boys died,
> they taught their father to understand contentment.
> Theirs was a Heaven-made filial piety,
> they were jewels among men.

Chatting with My Mother

(Gensei's mother died in the last month of 1667 at the age of 86.)

In the first month of summer in the year with the cyclical sign *hinoto-hitsuji* (1667), I spent the first three days with my mother. She said to me, "I've lived a great many years but I've never once had any desire to sit around doing nothing. And I think you're the same as me in that respect."

I laughed and replied, "I've heard that children who are born at night take after their mothers. I was born at night, wasn't I?"

"Yes," she said. "I gave birth to you on the night of the twenty-third day of the second month. I went out somewhere during the day. Then I came home, and around midnight, before I knew what was happening, I had given birth. The old woman from Sanuki was at my side and she bit the umbilical cord in two with her teeth and prayed you would have a long life. So I'm sure you're going to live for a long time!"

We chatted away happily until evening.

A Letter to Emyō

(Written from Takatsuki, where Gensei had gone in the last month of 1667 for treatment. Not long after writing this, he gave up the treatment and returned to his temple to die. Emyō was his chief disciple.)

The apprentice monk has arrived with news that all is well with you at the temple. Just hearing it, I fell a little less sick. And everything on the list of things you sent is right here before me. Receiving seven packets of thin incense makes me feel like a poor boy who has suddenly come into a fortune—I can't stop dancing for joy. And the hemp cloth I am having made up into a robe at once so I can change it for my cotton robe. It will be as light as the filmy garments worn by the gods in heaven and I know will help me greatly in getting over my fatigue.

During the past two days I have received a total of 350 acupuncture treatments and the great devil of sickness is in full retreat. But someone who was more than nine parts dead can't be so quickly brought back to life. So we win a battle and then lose a battle and the situation keeps changing day and night. It's like the serpent of Mount Ch'ang—if you attack the head the tail comes at you, and if you attack the tail the head comes at you. Very wearying, I can tell you! . . .

As for food, I still can't manage anything more than gruel, and that very thin with little grain and a lot of liquid. I spend a good deal of time with the evening lamp, but I must confess that of the morning, noon, and evening meals, only the evening meal has any real taste for me.

Alas, I'm afraid that if I go on breaking the rules of monastic discipline, I will never be rescued from this illness.[1] But since last summer when my illness broke out,

---

1. Monastic discipline required that one eat only two meals a day, fasting from noon on. The rule was often ignored in practice, but Gensei evidently observed it when his health permitted.

there are a great many days when I've broken the fast and few when I've kept it. Violating the rules of a monk like this, how can I help feeling shame and remorse!

As monks, we are engaged in a deeply serious endeavor, and what is needed in such an endeavor is to prevent illnes before it gets started. Now I know how true that is, and I pass the word on to you. When people talk about learning through your own illness to sympathize with the illnesses of others, I'm sure this is what they mean.

There are countless other things I'd like to write to you, but just writing this much I've had to lay down the brush any number of times and rest. So the other minor matters I will explain to the apprentice monk and let him tell you about them.

APPENDIX

Gensei's Japanese Poetry

The *Kunshūshū*, a short collection of notes by Gensei's disciple Emyō, indicates that Gensei, probably when he was around the age of nine, studied Japanese poetry under the famous poet Matsunaga Teitoku (1571–1653), who lived not far away from him in Kyoto.[1] Gensei himself states, however, that although he had been fond of Japanese poetry from his youth, he never studied with a teacher (*SZS* ch. 1, p. 32). I do not know how to explain this discrepancy, unless Gensei felt he had been too young when he studied under Teitoku to call himself a proper disciple. Gensei's *waka* or poems in Japanese have been generally admired, though they are certainly less original than his works in Chinese. I have translated a few examples here to give an idea of what his Japanese poetry is like and to demonstrate the way in which he at times treated a particular theme in both Chinese and Japanese.

In addition to studying and writing traditional style Japanese poetry, Gensei had a wide knowledge of the classics of Japanese literature. He was particularly fond of the *Tale of Genji* and is reported to have lectured on it to such eminent literary men as Kada

---

1. See Munemasa Isoo, "*Gensei—sono shutsuji*," in his *Nihon kinsei bun'en no kenkyū* (Tokyo: Miraisha, 1977), p. 33. On Gensei's *waka*, see Munemasa, "*Gensei*," *Bungagku gogaku* no. 58 (December 1970), pp. 69–78.

Nobuyuki, Kitamura Kigin, and the Confucian scholar Kumazawa Banzan.

1.
Tabi no sora
nani ka wabishiki
yo o sutete
idenishi mi ni wa
furusato mo nashi

Journey
The sky on a journey
looks somehow sad—
now that I've turned
my back on the world,
there's nowhere I call my home

2.
Ike no omo wa
yowa no arashi ni
tojihatete
matsu ni nokoreru
nami no oto kana

Ice
In the midnight storm
the pond's surface
has been sealed in ice,
but the sound of its waves
lingers in the pines

3.
Sato no inu no
ato no mi miete
furu yuki mo
itodo fukakusa
fuyu zo sabisihki

Morning after a Snowfall
All you can see
are tracks of village dogs—
snow piled up so deep
in Fukakusa,
winter's lonely!

4.
Uchinabiku
kozue ni miete
aoyagi no
ito yori hosoki
haru no mikazuki

Spring Poem
In wavering treetops
we see it,
slimmer than a frond
of green willow,
the crescent moon of spring

5.
Mine no kumo
tani no kasumi ni
kuchinu beshi
ukiyo no somenu
asa no sagoromo

Song of a Mountain Home
Among clouds of the peak,
valley mists,
I will grow old
never soiling these hemp robes
in the dusty world

6.   (To someone going to eastern Japan)
Ōkata no   Out in the world
yo ni nigoru to mo   you'll get muddy enough,
suminareshi   but our mountain waters
waga yama mizu no   where you used to live—
kokoro wasuru na   never forget that heart!

7. On a rainy day I visited the Byōdō-in and, spreading something to sit on by the main hall, remained there for a long time. I heard the distant tone of a bell, and when I asked where it came from, I was told it was the bell of Mimuro. (On the Byōdō-in, see p. 46. Mimuro is the site of another temple in the vicinity.)

Hakanakute   This brief day too
kyō mo kurekeri   has slipped away,
asu shiranu   and where will tomorrow find me?
Mimuro no yama no   From Mimuro hill,
iriai no kane   the evening bell

8.   *Resting on the Bridge*
Urayamashi   I envy you,
Uji no hashimori   guardian of the Uji bridge—
iku aki shi   how many autumns
tsuki o nagamete   have you seen such moons
toshi no henuramu   as the years went by!

9.   *In a House Where My Father*
                         Lived a Long Time
Fumiwakuru   This waste
ato wa mukashi no   I push my way through
niwa no omo ni   was once the garden,
tada na mo shiranu   now overgrown with grasses
kusa zo shigereru   I couldn't even name

10. The lotuses at Tō-ji are now at their best, so early in the morning I set off to see them, coming back over the Kamo River in the evening.

Natsu no hi no   I never even felt
atsusa mo shirazu   the heat of the summer day—
asagawa ya   going and coming,
yūgawa wataru   my way took me over
michi no yukiki wa   a morning river, an evening river

11.
Oshikaranu
mi zo oshimaruru
tarachine no
oya no nokoseru
katami to moeba

After the Death of My Mother
This body means nothing to me,
but when I think of it
as a remembrance from one
who meant so much,
my mother of the sagging breasts—

Translations From the Oriental Classics

Major Plays of Chikamatsu, tr. Donald Keene
Four Major Plays of Chikamatsu, tr. Donald Keene. Paperback text edition. 1961
Records of the Grand Historian of China, translated from the Shih chi of Ssu-ma Ch'ien, tr. Burton Watson, 2 vols. 1961
Instructions for Practical Living and Other Neo-Confucian Writings by Wang Yang-ming, tr. Wing-tsit Chan 1963
Chuang Tzu: Basic Writings, tr. Burton Watson, paperback ed. only 1964
The Mahābhārata, tr. Chakravarthi V. Narasimhan. Also in paperback ed. 1965
The Manyōshū, Nippon Gakujutsu Shinkōkai edition 1954
Su Tung-p'o: Selections from a Sung Dynasty Poet, tr. Burton Watson. Also in paperback ed. 1965
Bhartrihari: Poems, tr. Barbara Stoler Miller. Also in paperback ed. 1967
Basic Writings of Mo Tzu, Hsün Tzu, and Han Fei Tzu, tr. Burton Watson. Also in separate paperback eds. 1967
The Awakening of Faith, attributed to Aśvaghosha, tr. Yoshito S. Hakeda. Also in paperback ed. 1967
Reflections on Things at Hand: The Neo-Confucian Anthology, comp. Chu Hsi and Lü Tsu-ch'ien, tr. Wing-tsit Chan 1967
The Platform Sutra of the Sixth Patriarch, tr. Philip B. Yampolsky. Also in paperback ed. 1967
Essays in Idleness: The Tsurezuregusa of Kenkō, tr. Donald Keene. Also in paperback ed. 1967

The Pillow Book of Sei Shōnagon, tr. Ivan Morris, 2 vols.	1967
Two Plays of Ancient India: The Little Clay Cart and the Minister's Seal, tr. J. A. B. van Buitenen	1968
The Complete Works of Chuang Tzu, tr. Burton Watson	1968
The Romance of the Western Chamber (Hsi Hsiang chi), tr. S. I. Hsiung. Also in paperback ed.	1968
The Manyōshū, Nippon Gakujutsu Shinkōkai edition. Paperback text edition.	1969
Records of the Historian: Chapters from the Shih chi of Ssu-ma Ch'ien. Paperback text edition, tr. Burton Watson	1969
Cold Mountain: 100 Poems by the T'ang Poet Han-shan, tr. Burton Watson. Also in paperback ed.	1970
Twenty Plays of the Nō Theatre, ed. Donald Keene. Also in paperback ed.	1970
Chūshingura: The Treasury of Loyal Retainers, tr. Donald Keene. Also in paperback ed.	1971
The Zen Master Hakuin: Selected Writings, tr. Philip B. Yampolsky	1971
Chinese Rhyme-Prose, tr. Burton Watson. Also in paperback ed.	1971
Kūkai: Major Works, tr. Yoshito S. Hakeda	1972
The Old Man Who Does as He Pleases: Selections from the Poetry and Prose of Lu Yu, tr. Burton Watson	1973
The Lion's Roar of Queen Śrīmālā, tr. Alex & Hideko Wayman	1974
Courtier and Commoner in Ancient China: Selections from the History of The Former Han by Pan Ku, tr. Burton Watson. Also in paperback ed.	1974
Japanese Literature in Chinese, Vol. I: Poetry and Prose in Chinese by Japanese Writers of the Early Period, tr. Burton Watson	1975
Japanese Literature in Chinese, Vol. II: Poetry and Prose in Chinese by Japanese Writers of the Later Period, tr. Burton Watson	1976
Scripture of the Lotus Blossom of the Fine Dharma, tr. Leon Hurvitz. Also in paperback ed.	1976
Love Song of the Dark Lord: Jayadeva's Gītagovinda, tr. Barbara Stoler Miller. Also in paperback ed. Cloth ed. includes critical text of the Sanskrit.	1977

Ryōkan: Zen Monk-Poet of Japan, tr. Burton Watson	1977
Calming the Mind and Discerning the Real: From the Lam rim chen mo of Tson-kha-pa, tr. Alex Wayman	1978
The Hermit and the Love-Thief: Sanskrit Poems of Bhartrihari and Bilhana, tr. Barbara Stoler Miller	1978
The Lute: Kao Ming's P'i-p'a chi, tr. Jean Mulligan. Also in paperback ed.	1980
A Chronicle of Gods and Sovereigns: Jinnō Shōtōki of Kitabatake Chikafusa, tr. H. Paul Varley	1980
Among the Flowers: The Hua-chien chi, tr. Lois Fusek	1982
Grass Hill: Poems and Prose by the Japanese Monk Gensei, tr. Burton Watson	1983

Studies in Oriental Culture

1. *The Ōnin War: History of Its Origins and Background with a Selective Translation of the Chronicle of Ōnin*, by H. Paul Varley — 1967
2. *Chinese Government in Ming Times: Seven Studies*, ed. Charles O. Hucker — 1969
3. *The Actors' Analects (Yakusha Rongo)*, ed. and tr. by Charles J. Dunn and Bunzō Torigoe — 1969
4. *Self and Society in Ming Thought*, by Wm. Theodore de Bary and the Conference on Ming Thought. Also in paperback ed. — 1970
5. *A History of Islamic Philosophy*, by Majid Fakhry — 1970
6. *Phantasies of a Love Thief: The Caurapañcāśikā Attributed to Bilhana*, by Barbara Stoler Miller — 1971
7. *Iqbal: Poet-Philosopher of Pakistan*, ed. Hafeez Malik — 1971
8. *The Golden Tradition: An Anthology of Urdu Poetry*, by Ahmed Ali. Also in paperback ed. — 1973
9. *Conquerors and Confucians: Aspects of Political Change in Late Yüan China*, by John W. Dardess — 1973
10. *The Unfolding of Neo-Confucianism*, by Wm. Theodore de Bary and the Conference on Seventeenth-Century Chinese Thought. Also in paperback ed. — 1975
11. *To Acquire Wisdom: The Way of Wang Yang-ming*, by Julia Ching — 1976
12. *Gods, Priests, and Warriors: The Bhṛgus of the Mahābhārata*, by Robert P. Goldman — 1977
13. *Mei Yao-ch'en and the Development of Early Sung Poetry*, by Jonathan Chaves — 1976
14. *The Legend of Semimaru, Blind Musician of Japan*, by Susan Matisoff — 1977

Companions To Asian Studies

Approaches to the Oriental Classics. ed. Wm. Theodore de Bary   1959
Early Chinese Literature, by Burton Watson. Also in paperback ed.   1962
Approaches to Asian Civilizations, ed. Wm. Theodore de Bary and Ainslie T. Embree   1964
The Classic Chinese Novel: A Critical Introduction, by C. T. Hsia. Also in paperback ed.   1968
Chinese Lyricism: Shih Poetry from the Second to the Twelfth Century, tr. Burton Watson. Also in paperback ed.   1971
A Syllabus of Indian Civilization, by Leonard A. Gordon and Barbara Stoler Miller   1971
Twentieth-Century Chinese Stories, ed. C. T. Hsia and Joseph S. M. Lau. Also in paperback ed.   1971
A Syllabus of Chinese Civilization, by J. Mason Gentzler, 2d ed.   1972
A Syllabus of Japanese Civilization, by H. Paul Varley, 2d ed.   1972
An Introduction to Chinese Civilization, ed. John Meskill, with the assistance of J. Mason Gentzler   1973
An Introduction to Japanese Civilization, ed. Arthur E. Tiedemann   1974
A Guide to Oriental Classics, ed. Wm. Theodore de Bary and Ainslie T. Embree, 2d ed. Also in paperback ed.   1975

Introduction To Oriental Civilizations

Wm. Theodore de Bary, Editor

Sources of Japanese Tradition	1958	Paperback ed., 2 vols.	1964
Sources of Indian Tradition	1958	Paperback ed., 2 vols.	1964
Sources of Chinese Tradition	1960	Paperback ed., 2 vols.	1964